A Fly on the RBI WALL

'Lucidly written and with a subtle sense of humour, Alpana has narrated the critical events in the history of RBI during the two decades in which period she was the head of the Communication Department. Her narration shows how good communication can enhance the image and credibility of the Institution. In this process, we also get to know more about the governors themselves! Worth reading by everyone.'

—C. Rangarajan
Former Governor, RBI

'"Central bank communication" was once considered an oxymoron; it has now turned into a fine art. Central bankers have discovered that effective communication can be a powerful policy tool, especially in crisis times. They have also learnt, much to their dismay, that a communication misstep can be hugely costly. This book is an engrossing portrayal of how the RBI has managed communication challenges over the last two decades. Anyone curious about what happens inside the RBI "black box" will find this book irresistible.'

—Duvvuri Subbarao
Former Governor, RBI

'As RBI's media handler, Alpana Killawala had two exacting roles to perform: to get the Bank's view across as effectively as possible and make the media believe it wasn't being neglected. In this book, she describes these varied, vexing and uplifting experiences as an insider, who enjoyed the confidence of the institution and its top management. This is a valuable addition to the growing literature on the history of the Bank. One can only say bon appétit.'

—T.C.A. Srinivasa Raghavan
Columnist

'In this engaging account, Alpana gives you something between a personal memoir and what one might call history between the lines. There is no shortage of anecdotes to keep the pages turning, served with insights on how communications could be a strategic asset to any organisation. Well worth a read.'

—T.N. Ninan
Chairman, *Business Standard*

A Fly on the RBI WALL

An Insider's View of the Central Bank

ALPANA KILLAWALA

RUPA

Published by
Rupa Publications India Pvt. Ltd 2024
7/16, Ansari Road, Daryaganj
New Delhi 110002

Sales centres:
Bengaluru Chennai
Hyderabad Jaipur Kathmandu
Kolkata Mumbai Prayagraj

P-ISBN: 978-93-5702-886-8
E-ISBN: 978-93-5702-928-5

Second impression 2024

10 9 8 7 6 5 4 3 2

Printed in India

Contents

Foreword

A foreword to a book generally captures an author's impressive personality, command over subject, details of interesting incidents and an occasional joke or two. The foreword to this book, *A Fly on the RBI Wall*, written by the Reserve Bank of India's (RBI) well-known communication officer, Alpana Killawala, is an exception, just as her admirable, informative, insightful account of the RBI is, both in style and substance.

The 1990s witnessed, among other things, economic reforms in India that changed the very fabric of the country's economy. The general feeling at that time was that the implementation of policies and programmes in India was very poor and, as such, required overhauling. Communication was a major missing link in this.

For central banks, which form an important part of a country's economy, however, this was a period when they were found to be moving away from their mysterious ways of communication to greater transparency. The RBI was, therefore, no exception in its desire to be more transparent, galvanized by the reform process undertaken by India at that time. Any account of this period will engage vast readership, as posterity will try to understand the process, people and institutions involved in India's metamorphosis.

Many governors and deputy governors have, in the past, written about their experiences rather elaborately. More recently, the RBI came out with the fifth volume of its official history titled *Reserve Bank of India, Volume 5, 1997–2008*. The volume is authored by a team of longstanding RBI officials, led by Dr Tirthankar Roy, a globally renowned professor of economic history. This official account gave me an opportunity to appreciate and gain a deeper understanding of the history of the central bank as related by a professor. In his introduction, Roy summarizes the institutional changes in the RBI during this period very effectively. He says:

> The Reserve Bank of India became a leaner, more dynamic and more outward looking organisation during the reference period, capable of handling a more diverse and challenging range of tasks with a smaller workforce. One of the ways this was achieved was by incentivising training and professionalism, restructuring the workforce, and making strategic changes in placement and recruitment policy. The Bank also began recruiting specialised staff on a contract basis, to meet the needs for few types of service.[1]

Describing the journey of the RBI in those crucial years of reforms, Professor Roy, in the particular context of communication, further says:

> Several old departments were either wound up or merged with other departments as their functions became redundant. The Bank also divested its ownership in subsidiaries and, at the same time, new departments were set up as the need arose. The Bank management, being conscious of the crucial role of communication in the conduct of its monetary, regulatory and supervisory

---

[1]Roy, Tirthankar, *Reserve Bank of India, Volume 5, 1997–2008*, Cambridge University Press, 2022, p. 12.

> initiatives focussed on enhancing the coverage quality and format of information dissemination. Both internal and external communication of the Bank received impetus during this period. Internal communication processes facilitated two-way communication and during the period of reference, were made more transparent. The Bank officials were encouraged to engage more closely with market participants with an emphasis on providing prompt response to the media and public.[2]

The introduction continues; the rest of the volume contains these changes in more details than is possible to discuss here. But 'the crucial role of communication' brings me to this book. I believe Alpana's book *A Fly on the RBI Wall* will be unique and worth reading, and I explain why.

Alpana was an early and one of the 'specialized staff' referred to by Roy in the official history of RBI, recruited from the market for specifically developing the communication function. She was a witness to the change that the economy and its most significant institution had gone through for almost a quarter of a century. And for this reason, Alpana's book gains importance. It rounds up a period of history almost coterminous with the economic reforms of India, with the RBI governors who were in charge as the focal point.

It has been said more than once that the RBI is a governor-centric organization. This book is unique in the sense that it captures from a staff member's point of view how each governor of the RBI left his imprint on the institution. Rather than competing with the official history of the central bank, this book engagingly narrates her own perception of the events of that time. In doing so, Alpana has provided a

---

[2]Ibid.

lot more details than can be found in the annual reports and autobiographies of governors and deputy governors on the working of central banks in relation to markets. What is commendable is that she does this without any pretence on her part and without offending the personalities she has written about, giving insights into institutional dynamics of the RBI. In fact, by giving an account of her journey, in describing the personalities involved and the interactions between them at a critical period in history when the reforms were taken and handled under crises, the book provides an insight into the remarkable capacities of people and their interactions within a complex organization.

Stylistically, the book brings out micro aspects, institutional dynamics, deep knowledge, sensitivity, patience, group dynamics, new ideas and, above all, a willingness to learn from professionals in different areas.

Again, this book is different inasmuch as it has an underlying theme of tracing the evolution of communication function in the RBI—from mere dissemination of information to transparency and two-way communication. The story of evolution of communication is, in fact, Alpana's story, as she was the one heading the communication function in the RBI through India's economic reforms and the central bank's evolution from a traditional, slow and staid institution to a lean and modern central bank raring to keep in step with the changing times.

That is why, those who miss to read Alpana Killawala's book would lose a valuable understanding of the institutional dynamics of an important institution like the Reserve Bank of India during a critical period of India's contemporary economic history.

Knowingly or unknowingly, the book also provides, as an aside, lessons in communication in general and central bank communication in particular, if one takes the anecdotes as practical examples for the communication strategies described. Alpana's book is thus different and makes reading it worthwhile.

I wish Alpana and her book the very best.

Y.V. Reddy
Former Governor, Reserve Bank of India

Preface

In a large, traditional and conservative institution like the Reserve Bank of India (RBI), it is easy to become a stereotype and spend your lifetime pushing papers back and forth. You will continue to receive your salary and promotions by doing just that. It is extremely difficult to be different, especially if you want to bring about any changes. The system doesn't accept you, nor does it easily accept changes. But if you try harder and be patient, it slowly starts responding, and then, at the other end of the tunnel, you can finally see light. The system as well as its people appreciate your efforts. The only condition is that you have to be a part of the system to change it; you cannot change it by remaining outside and merely criticizing it.

When I joined the RBI in June 1992 as a deputy general manager in the RBI's Press Relations Division—as it was known at that time—like most other young people, I was starry-eyed and wanted to change the entire institution. Within no time, I learnt how foolish that dream was. Leave apart the institution, I understood in the very first year of my career in the RBI that if I could even bring in some change in my area of operation, it would be a great achievement. That's what S.S. Tarapore, the deputy governor of the RBI between January 1992 and September 1996 and my mentor in the RBI, would tell me whenever I felt frustrated. Over the next 26 years or so, I tried just that—to bring a little bit of change in the world around me.

I won some and lost many. But the way we communicated by the time I had to hang my boots was visibly different from what it was when I had joined. Well, some would say I was 'instrumental' in bringing about a change in the way we communicated. I would say that I happened to be in the right place at the right time. And well, I also happened to be the right person; just as Dr Bimal Jalan, governor of the RBI between November 1997 and September 2003, told me before he left, 'Your being there helped.'

I was a journalist prior to joining the RBI and wrote primarily on banking, finance and the RBI. My job required me to interact with several senior banking professionals including the RBI governor. I had spoken with S. Venkitaramanan at various functions. He served as the RBI governor from December 1990 to December 1992. Reportedly, he suggested that someone like me should be recruited in the Press Relations Division to develop the communication function. The RBI followed due process—from advertising the post to inviting applications and then conducting a written test as well as an interview—for the recruitment. I joined the organization as a regular employee.

Throughout my time there, I could remain a journalist at heart. I managed to retain—well, to a large extent—my language, behaviour, stance and curiosity. It was, of course, partly a conscious effort on my part. I was hoping to return to journalism one day. But thanks to this attitude, I could closely and objectively observe the institution, its people and its system. While working there, I had a ringside view of many important events that changed the course of banking, finance and the economy. Many of these events were a crisis; and as we got over the crisis, the institutional response to it had resulted in the changing of the institution too—bit by bit. 'One chip at a time', as the saying goes.

I have been fortunate to have lived through the evolution of the institution from June 1992 to February 2019. And that is what I have tried to capture in this book—the evolution of the RBI through the eyes of an insider who used to be an outsider. I have no ambition or illusion of contributing to the history of the institution or to the economic history of this country through this book. My vision in attempting to jot down my learnings is limited to my functional area—communication. I have also tried to capture the evolution of the institution and, while doing so, may have captured a glimpse of the personalities behind the change through the lens of communication. As such, wherever I have tried to report the events, they may, at times, appear to be of a slightly different hue than those recorded in official history. I suggest the reader may go by the official history for accuracy.

The RBI faced some major and minor crises during my tenure. The 1991 balance of payments (BOP) crisis, the Harshad Mehta scam, India's economic reforms, the 1997 Asian crisis, the 1998 Russian crisis, the Ketan Parekh scam, reforms in the government securities market, the 2007–8 global financial crisis and, finally, the 2016 demonetization. These are just some events off the top of my head. The overarching phenomenon, however, was the decade of reforms—India changing the path of its economic development. From a planned economy, it shifted gears to become a market economy. From control, it moved to liberalization and management. So huge was this change that it required a complete shift in the mindset of the nation. I would say that the change hasn't got fully absorbed even today.

The anecdotes in the book are in first-person singular. Initially I tried to avoid this, since, in such a large institution, no single person can claim to do anything single-handedly. At the same time, I have also learnt that the person in the seat does matter. If P.V. Narasimha Rao, Dr Manmohan Singh and C. Rangarajan were not at the helm of affairs, the face of India's economic reforms would have been different. The anecdotes try to illustrate this. Somewhere through the daily routine, the communication function evolved and there were lessons that I learnt. These lessons stayed with me. After retiring from the RBI, one of my occupations has been teaching communication to younger generations. As I was using some of these anecdotes as illustrations while teaching, I realized that they were, after all, not so insignificant. This gave me confidence to jot them down as my two-bit contribution to the literature on communication.

I may seem a little disappointed once in a while through the narration. But it is only natural. As in any job, I too faced ups and downs. But the overall experience is unforgettable, fulfilling and satisfying. Working closely with six stalwart governors of the RBI was by itself an exhilarating experience. And I would say that I could bring in whatever change I did in the area of communication because I always had the ear of the incumbent governor. I firmly believe today that communication should be a strategic function and not a residual one.

Hope you enjoy reading this different take on the institution that is the Reserve Bank of India.

1

S. Venkitaramanan

First Wind of Change

The RBI was not new to me. I was well versed in the functioning of the central bank. I had met R.N. Malhotra, predecessor to Governor S. Venkitaramanan, before. I was 'the journalist who had interviewed the governor'; that is how people recognized me in my early days at the RBI. I was perhaps the only journalist in a long time to have met the RBI governor and to have interviewed him. The junior-level RBI employees looked at me with awe. In reality, the interview was a virtual washout. The governor's office had asked me for a questionnaire. I had sent a list of some 15–20 questions asking him everything under the sun. Later, when I was setting up interviews of journalists with the governors, I would get frustrated with their tendency to ask 'everything under the sun!' It is only now that I appreciate this. You don't get to meet and interview the RBI governor every day. And so the idea is to make the best out of the opportunity and get as much as possible. To my surprise, when I entered Malhotra's office, after the initial pleasantries he handed over the text of prepared answers to all my questions. There was nothing left to talk about. For a moment, I wondered what to do. But my slot was for one hour, and I decided that I would not give that up. So, I sat through and just chatted with him.

Malhotra was a man of few words and did not easily show his emotions. Still, in that one-hour chat, I could sense his pain about the government not listening to the RBI. At that time, apart from fiscal deficits, the bone of contention between the two institutions was the farm-loan waivers. The issue of the farm-loan waivers was a favourite subject of the then minister of state for finance. The RBI was against the idea, as loan waivers vitiated the credit culture. Simply speaking, this meant that the good borrower who paid up his loan instalments regularly would have no incentive to repay his loan, because his counterpart who did not pay got his loan waived after some time! And once the borrower tasted blood in the form of the loan waiver, he would want it again and again. And if all the people stopped repaying their loans, how would the banking system function? The government, with an eye on elections, was hell-bent on announcing a loan waiver for the farmers. Soon after the interview was published, the then state minister of finance announced the waiver, and Malhotra put in his papers. My article was in no way responsible for his resignation. But I was not surprised, as I had, so to say, seen it coming. After this episode, I continued to visit the RBI occasionally and met whoever was willing to meet journalists—not many were!—to understand its policies.

How I Got Started

S. Venkitaramanan was the governor of the RBI for two brief years (1990–1992). He was largely instrumental in bringing about a little change in the way the Bank worked—to be nimble on its feet. In bringing me, a working journalist, into the RBI, his objective was to professionalize the press relations function. My joining the Bank was the first manifestation of the change he wanted to bring in the institution. As a journalist who covered banking, finance and the RBI for *Business India*, a fortnightly business magazine, I would often call the RBI governor's office and put in a request for an appointment. But the governor's office never got back with an appointment. Once, I met Governor Venkitaramanan at a public function. I simply mentioned his office not getting back to me. He was surprised that his office never reverted to me; at the same time, he also gave me another number, telling me that the lady on that number would give me the appointment. Later, I came to know that it was commonplace in the RBI to directly reject any journalist's request at the secretarial level. When I called that number, I did get the appointment I was seeking. After that, I could call him any time I wanted to, and he would chat with me with ease—sharing news as well as views.

Unknown to me, perhaps my chats with him made him tell his colleagues in the Bank that they should get someone like me to manage the RBI's press relations function. I entered the RBI a full year after that, but only after fulfilling all the procedural requirements. The post was officially advertised and I was persuaded by some senior officials of the RBI to at least apply. I took their advice and, after a written test and an interview by the Bank's recruitment board, got selected for the post. I was told later that there were more than 10 aspirants along with me for that job and that I stood first in the test and interview scores, and if the rest of the candidates were to be ranked, the rank would have to start from number 10.

Anyway, I entered the RBI as an employee in June 1992 in the midst of the 1991 BOP crisis and the Harshad Mehta scam. It was interesting, as I had covered both the crises as a journalist, and, now, I was getting the opportunity to see from within how the RBI was dealing with them.

Bold Steps

Venkitaramanan was appointed the governor when the 1991 BOP criris hit the country. The RBI had imposed a 200 per cent margin requirement on bank finance for imports. This was to save the scanty foreign exchange from draining out. The banking system and the industry were in shock. We had to pledge some of our gold to the Bank of England to get a small loan to tide over the crisis. I had written about it in a cover story for *Business India.* It was my last cover story for the magazine.

Mortgaging the jewellery to resolve a financial crisis is the last thing a family would do in India. Pledging the country's gold was like mortgaging one's family jewels to tide over the debt problem. It was—and is—a complete taboo. Venkitaramanan always thought out of the box. He suggested pledging the gold was much better than defaulting on international debt repayment. There are stories in public domain about how he managed to convince the government to do this despite tough opposition and how the van that carried the gold to be transported to London developed some snag on the way to the airport and that a journalist got wind of it. It was Venkitaramanan who spoke to the editor of the newspaper and requested that the story be held up just for a day so that the gold could successfully be transported out of the country. This was my first lesson in central bank communication. We never ever prevented a story from publishing.

By the time I joined, much of the work on the BOP front was already done, and India was on its way to recovery and reform. Regardless, I happened to be privy to one conversation. I was sitting in front of Governor Venkitaramanan—now as an employee of the Reserve Bank—when there was an external call. I started to leave but the governor gestured at me asking me to wait. Since I was right there, I could hear what he was saying. He usually spoke very softly. I could barely get the conversation. After disconnecting the phone, he made a quick internal call and told someone that the Bank of Japan had agreed to give us some loan and that the person on the other end of the phone should follow it through.

Later, I figured out that the call was from someone at the Bank of Japan who conveyed that the Bank had agreed to give a small loan in Japanese Yen to India. Yes, we were so desperate that we took every small loan that added some foreign exchange to our kitty. I wonder if any other person in that seat could have done this—a loan of a few million Japanese Yen to a country that, only a few days back, was on the verge of defaulting on its repayment obligation! Of course, we had subsequent governors of the likes of Dr Y.V. Reddy who were extremely well-connected. But, by then, there were international forums like the Bank for International Settlements (BIS) and the International Monetary Fund (IMF) which had started doing regular bi-monthly meetings, where the heads of various central banks of the world would meet and discuss issues. These regular meetings helped build relationships.

The Difference

Venkitaramanan was different as an RBI governor from his predecessors. All the governors till then, including Malhotra, were traditional and conservative. But Venkitaramanan was a non-conformist and worked at breakneck speed. Unfortunately, he got caught in many controversies. He was perceived to be close to one particular industry house. I do not know if he really was, but that did not come in the way, as far as his role in the

RBI was concerned. The media also wanted him to bear the cross of failing to regulate banks in the Harshad Mehta scam. Little did they know that had it not been for him, the scam would have continued for many more years. Moreover, the 1991 BOP crisis and Venkitaramanan's role in getting the country to tide over that crisis was also conveniently sidelined by them.

Having joined the RBI, I quickly got involved in media-related work. The governor was quick-witted and had a sharp sense of humour. He was very swift and therefore impatient in his work. His office was on the eighteenth floor while mine was on the twenty-third. He would call me and assign a task to me. Being young, I would run up five floors to my office to carry out the task. But no sooner had I reached my office than I would receive a call from him on my intercom that he had completed the said task. He believed in no hierarchy and would walk on to any floor just so that he could discuss issues with the people actually handling that work. He kept a close watch on what the media wrote and also had his ear to the ground. Unlike his predecessors, he received a lot of market gossip. He had the ability to join the pieces together and make the full story. That is how the Harshad Mehta scam was unearthed. It was, in fact, the RBI, nay Venkitaramanan, who could understand the link between trading in bankers' receipts (BRs) and the rising stock market, which is what Harshad Mehta was doing—borrowing money from banks through BRs and investing it in '*badla*' in the stock market and returning the money to banks two days later when the badla would unwind.

It was Venkitaramanan who saw through the unholy connection between the government securities market and the stock market going on for many years. Trading in BRs was against the law and had to be stopped. But stopping it was not easy. He would be taking the bull by its horn. After all, Harshad Mehta was nicknamed 'The Big Bull' by the media.

The Harshad Mehta scam had spilled over in the public domain by the time I joined the RBI, and the media was chasing it, breaking one or more stories on a daily basis. I, too, had done my bit in covering the scam as a journalist. I had written one story explaining how the market was trading in BRs, which were mere paper with no backing of securities, and raising money against them only to invest in the stock market. I wrote in my story, among other things, that the RBI was looking into the trading of BRs issued on the back of government securities. In the last sentence of my story, I had said that the practice of issuing BRs was going on at a much larger scale in public sector bonds and the Unit Scheme 1964 (US '64 or US-64) issued by the Unit Trust of India (UTI). Later, the governor expressed regret about not paying heed to what I had said in my article. He told me more than once even after he left the RBI that 'I wish I had listened to you at that time.' Investigations had revealed that BRs were issued not only against non-existent government securities but also against non-existent PSU bonds and US '64. That part of the scam turned out to be a huge corporate fraud done by a foreign bank using a small private sector bank and a broker. That's what the governor kept referring to.

Unfortunately, the media blamed the RBI for the Harshad Mehta scam. This certainly was not entirely true, as the documents revealed that the RBI knew about the malpractice of trading in BRs for nearly a decade, and its inspectors were pointing it out in their inspection reports which went all the way up to the deputy governor in charge of banking regulation. But after that nothing happened. When Venkitaramanan took over as the governor and got to know this, he decided to put a stop to the practice even if it was an 'accepted market practice'. It was legally not allowed, he argued, and the regulator could not allow an illegal practice to continue after knowing about it, even if it were an 'accepted market practice'.

Trying to Pass the Buck

For me, a journalist, joining the RBI during the Harshad Mehta scam was indeed a golden opportunity. My first intention was to see all the papers myself, meet as many officials as possible within the Bank dealing with the investigation and find out the truth—a journalist's utopia. This was not very difficult as, by the time I joined the Bank, the Janakiraman Committee—with R. Janakiraman, one of the deputy governors of the RBI, as its chairman—had already been set up to investigate securities irregularities and was at work. The government, too, had set up a Joint Parliamentary Committee (JPC) to look into the scam. While the Janakiraman Committee did all the technical work of unravelling the complex deals, the JPC looked for scapegoats. The RBI departments were working overtime to feed information and documents to both these committees.

Unknown to the public, Venkitaramanan had set up an informal committee of a few young officers of the RBI to coordinate and organize (read: strategize) communication with JPC, including organizing information and documents to be supplied to both these committees. The governor quickly but informally made me a part of this group. My role was mainly to give an outsider's view to this internal committee and help strategize communication. This gave me access to a lot of information which existed in the RBI about the irregularities and led me to the conviction that the RBI was not the culprit.

The agenda of both these committees were seemingly the same, but the way both functioned was very different. The Janakiraman Committee was a technical committee that looked into the modus operandi and the dramatis personae in the scandal. The reports of this committee formed the basis of investigation by the JPC and were later used extensively by the courts of law while dealing with the numerous court cases relating to the scam.

Janakiraman, the chairman of the committee, had a diminutive figure and was god-fearing. He was solid knowledge-wise, yet was extremely soft-spoken, straightforward and respectful of everyone. The report of this committee, which came out in several parts, was full of details of how the banks and the brokers took advantage of lacunae in the manual system. The committee made several constructive recommendations to prevent the reoccurrence of such a scam in the securities market, the most important recommendation being computerization of the entire function. Computerization was something that the RBI would have never been able to do on its own, as the employees' unions were opposing it tooth and nail.

The JPC's task was the same—to find out what went wrong and how. However, it took it upon itself to punish the culprits too. It was a committee of politicians and, naturally, did not know the complexities of the securities market. It did not understand the way the loopholes had been exploited. So, it completely depended on the Janakiraman Committee reports for details. The JPC also informally took help of some journalists and players in the securities market to understand the technicalities involved in the transactions. However, their entire objective seemed to be to find scapegoats. While the court of law would take care of the scamsters, rolling heads from within the system—in particular, from the RBI—was the unwritten task of JPC. They were looking for some people in the banks and the RBI to take the blame, and, with media in tow, the RBI governor was a big fish they wanted to catch.

Building Bridges—Within and Without

Perhaps Venkitaramanan had got a whiff of it, though he never explicitly told me so. But, within a week of my joining, he told me to take ₹10,000 from the RBI—at that this was a good amount—and go to Delhi, meet my journalist friends and find out what was happening. Barely seven days into the job, I had no idea about the RBI rules and procedure of arranging for the travel, stay and meetings. More importantly, how exactly to 'take ₹10,000' from the RBI? My mentor, Deputy Governor Tarapore, in charge of the Press Relations Division, of which I was appointed the head, came to my aid. I had known him even before joining the RBI, and here he had kindly taken me under his wings. He heard me stoically (now I can sense him laughing loudly in his mind at my naivety) and then told me in his typical baritone voice to not do 'any such thing' in the RBI—meaning taking cash worth ₹10,000. He told me to meet a particular officer in the human resources (HR) department and take guidance.

The HR lady gave me an important life lesson. She told me that if I wanted to survive in the system, I should follow the system and not bypass it by dropping the governor's name. For me this was forever a dilemma—whether to follow the system and accept the delay in decision-making or to follow the governor's orders and, while doing so, bypass the hierarchy. As a protector of RBI's reputation, which was the role assigned to me directly or indirectly, I often had to directly take orders from the governor. Sometimes, in doing so, I had to face the wrath of the system. But I did learn the lesson well and tried taking this path sparingly. Governors come and go, the RBI is permanent. Neither then, nor any time later, did I use the governor's name in the RBI. But the incident, perhaps, set the RBI thinking for the first time about an 'entertainment allowance' for the spokesperson of the Bank. Beginning with ₹10,000 in 1992, now the RBI pays a handsome entertainment allowance to all its senior officers, helping them inasmuch as they can to now afford to pay for a meal with a banker or a mediaperson in case the need arises.

It was a small amount at that time, and, to be honest, I didn't require even that much—during my entire career combined. In any case, the RBI wouldn't have paid for alcohol—the major part of the meal cost. I used to instead invite journalists home for a meal, so the treat would be on me. And when I would meet someone outside, most of the time, the journalist would pay, as almost all of them were peers and, therefore, friends first. Perhaps, they thought that the RBI did not pay me any entertainment allowance or paid very little (which was true). Somewhere, the respect they had for the RBI also worked in my favour. The result was that I never needed to pay much attention to this aspect and the entertainment allowance remained small. Maybe I should have worked a little more on this front to make the life of future incumbents in the department slightly better.

Going to Delhi as an RBI officer was a new experience for me. The allowance I got towards lodging and boarding was so small that I could not find any decent hotel to stay in Delhi in that amount. The office, however, did put me up in a centrally-located hotel. When my journalist friends got to know where the hotel was, one of them warned me not to open my bags but wait for him at the reception. He came instantly and whisked me away from there, taking me to his house. Upon reaching his place, he told me that the hotel I was put up in was infamous as a 'pick-up' joint. The RBI as an institution lived in its own world and would have had no idea about this, I am sure. So, I stayed in an extra room in a journalist's house and tried to find out what Delhi journalists were up to in the matter of the JPC! Ironical as it sounds now, at that time, I didn't have any qualms, as for me they were all friends, not adversaries. During the day, when my friend would go out on his appointments, I would sit in his house and call up journalists to know what was happening. I would also call up Venkitaramanan to brief him on what Delhi was up to. I personally knew only a handful of journalists in Delhi. Friends helped me out in getting to know others. The RBI name opened up many doors too. Soon, I started meeting them on my own.

I quickly realized that the Delhi media had an agenda. This was so perhaps because Delhi is a power centre, and politicians and journalists use each other for their advantage. I came to learn that the Delhi journalists had decided that the governor's head would roll in the Harshad Mehta scam.

My Delhi visits that were, by now, once every week, were packed with meetings with journalists, trying to convince them about the governor's work in the RBI and the positive role he had played in unearthing the scam. I was meeting the editors as well as ground-level reporters in their offices and even in the press club. Unknowingly, I had started educating the journalists on the way the RBI functioned. Slowly, the conversations started becoming less heated and journalists started listening to me. I would show them the papers that I had seen and that had convinced me that the RBI *was* and *should be* the prosecutor and not the prosecuted. Yet, they did not or could not give up on Venkitaramanan. I have a very faint memory of Venkitaramanan telling someone that he should at least get to complete his term. One, he had a very short tenure anyway and, two, to let him go before completing even that—that would be so uncharitable to a governor who not only had boldly pulled the country out of the 1991 BOP crisis but also was actually responsible for unearthing the scam.

I was continuously thinking of ways to get the media to understand how the RBI functioned. This was important in the wake of the scam, as the media had no idea about the process of inspecting banks and what happens next. N.D. Parameswaran, who was the chief of the banking operations department—at that time bank regulation and supervision were not two separate functions—was a known RBI official. He was a chain-smoker. I had met him earlier as a journalist and we had often spoken at length about the scam and the RBI. So impressed was I with his knowledge and attitude towards work that I requested him to take a session with the journalists—perhaps the first ever in the RBI.

I suggested to him that we meet the journalists informally and brief them about bank regulations and supervision in general, and, this way, they would understand that the RBI was the prosecutor. He suggested that we meet at my official residence, which, by now, had been allocated to me. Neither the chief of banking regulations nor I had the intention to do the informal session with the journalists keeping the governor in the dark. So, we both independently kept him in the loop without telling each other. Sometime later, I had asked Parameswaran if he had kept the governor informed; he had responded with a yes. Extremely relieved to know that, I told him that I too had kept him informed, and we both laughed.

This was a novel experiment in the RBI. I did not have enough experience to know or be afraid of the repercussions of such an experiment. The session obviously was completely off-the-record. I got all the journalists to take an oath of secrecy, as I was afraid that someone would write about it and would get both Parameswaran and me in trouble. In that session, Parameswaran informally spoke to the journalists non-stop for three hours or so. I don't remember the details of the talk but it was partly about bank regulations in general and partly about the Harshad Mehta scam. What I also remember is that, for three hours, the journalists were just spellbound. Somehow, I could not arrange such sessions again until Y.V. Reddy took over as the governor and encouraged me to conduct training sessions for the journalists.

An Aside

The story of Harshad Mehta had a sad ending. Not only did he die in jail but some of his contemporaries who were named in securities irregularities also met with a similar fate. M.J. Pherwani, chairman of UTI; B. Ratnakar, chairman of Canara Bank; the treasury incharges of State Bank of India (SBI) and the Discount and Finance House of India (DFHI) died as well.[1] They were all involved in the securities scam. Some others, like the treasury in charge and two of his ace traders in Citibank, just disappeared from the Indian scene; there were stories floating about the whereabouts of the Citibank treasury head but no one could confirm the details. Even others, like associates of Harshad Mehta and Bhupen Dalal, served a long and miserable term in jail.

Unlike in the developed world, we do not have laws against

---

[1] '"Mystery" Deaths in Scandals", *The Telegraph*, 16 March 2011, https:// tinyurl.com/3enh2zvh. Accessed on 24 January 2024; Deshpande, Swati, '5 Convicted in ₹1,700 Crore Fraud; 3 Others Acquitted', *The Times of India*, 8 July 2018, https://tinyurl.com/ey42adt8. Accessed on 24 January 2024.

financial crime. Nick Leeson, the rogue English derivatives trader who started his career around the same time as Harshad Mehta, in 1991–92, indulged in risky trades causing Barings Bank to go bankrupt by 1995. But when he was caught, he was quickly put through a trial and given a 6.5-year term in jail and was released in 1999 on medical grounds. He lived a normal life after that. In India, since we do not have laws against financial crime, it is difficult to book the criminal under any law, to begin with. Most of them are booked for some related but smaller crimes under civil law, such as cheque bouncing. The law—especially civil law—takes excruciatingly long for the culprit to be booked and punished. Cheque-bouncing cases used to take two to five years to even come before the court of law, prior to it becoming a criminal offence. In the meantime, some of the accused die, some get released on bail and live a happily-ever-after life, some run away from the country just so that they don't have to face that long-winding trial that goes nowhere, some live a life of anonymity. Only very few are prosecuted and have to serve their term miserably in jail.

Getting the House in Order

Venkitaramanan was one governor who thought about the future of the RBI as an institution. As India moved from controls to liberalization, it was necessary to change the mindset of its employees, who were its most valuable asset. He appointed Arthur Anderson, a well-known multinational management firm of that time, to prepare a strategic action plan for the Bank. A team of young officers (young, at that time, meant people in their 40s and 50s) assisted the team of Arthur Anderson. The representatives of the firm, as far as I remember, were all novices. They went from department to department, met the heads and asked them for their vision. The reports were compiled to make the firm's report.

I was a fresh entrant trying to find my own feet. My role was not yet in the limelight. Naturally, no one concerned with that report took notice of a small division like the Press Relations Division, when it was among the rising functions per the governor's vision. I expressed my disappointment about this to someone in the internal team coordinating the work, and, with the governor's support, I got my first opportunity to articulate my vision of the function.

Today, I don't remember what I had said and what the team of Arthur Anderson had written. The report, too, got buried, as the media, in its tirade against Venkitaramanan, also criticized him for appointing a 'foreign firm' as an advisor to the Bank. This was quite unnecessary; reforming the institution was as important as reforming the country's economy. Unfortunately, no one in the RBI bothered to keep it alive. It was typical of the institution, where once a governor left, his priorities were quickly forgotten, and the new governor's priorities were hastily adopted. The next real effort to reform the institution came only after 21 years in 2013, when Dr Raghuram Rajan took it upon himself to restructure the institution.

Communication Function and Hierarchy

Working closely with the governors was an advantage as well as a disadvantage. The RBI also had an uncanny sense of knowing who was the 'favourite' of the governor and who wasn't—basically, who the governor liked to work directly with and who were the ones he left to others to deal with. The collective attitude towards the employee would quickly change accordingly. In a hierarchical organization it is difficult for others to appreciate that the communication of any organization has to be shaped by its chief executive, and, therefore, it is of utmost importance that the communication head works closely with the head of the institution.

Venkitaramanan understood communication. That is how I got recruited in the first place—to shape the communication function. He would directly call me to discuss strategies and to give me instructions even if, hierarchically, I had a reporting line comprising the secretary to the RBI's board of directors, an executive director and a deputy governor. I would get to meet the governor almost every day and sometimes even more than once in a day. He would also ring me up over the weekends to discuss news articles and whether and how that would affect the RBI or him. The RBI, being a hierarchical institution, always found it difficult to accept that an officer of the rank of deputy general manager like me could get a direct call from the governor. Some seniors understood this and were tolerant; others didn't and waited till the governor left the institution so that they could 'put me in my place'. I was fortunate. Governor after governor paid attention to communication inasmuch as they left me alone to design it the way I thought right. I suffered ill-luck only twice during my tenure!

Deputy Governor Tarapore understood both—the need for the governor to directly give me instructions and the need to observe hierarchical balance. He had risen through the ranks to become the deputy governor. He understood the RBI's psyche extremely well. He would constantly sensitize me that Venkitaramanan's way of working was different and that I should not expect to be so closely associated with the governors after him. In fact, he guided me on how to find a way and carry out the governor's instructions through the system. I would try to do this but it wasn't always possible, due to which I did suffer because I 'did not keep the hierarchy informed'.

Building Camaraderie Within

There were many odds against me. I was young—in my early thirties—when I joined the RBI. I had joined straight in the senior management cadre, in grade 'D', which was the first step of senior management. The average age of grade 'D' in the RBI at that time was over 50. I had a clear 20-year advantage over them if I were to compete with them for promotion. I was also perceived as one of the media—even if now I was a part of the RBI. Media in the RBI was shunned before I joined. Naturally, they would not open up to me. For quite a long while, the RBI officials would shut up or change the topic at the lunch table as soon as I would enter the room or tried to join the conversation. I would feel hurt about this, and once, much later, I said so to a group of very senior officials who, in a get-together, were standing and gossiping about something. It hurt because I lost out on gossip which is essential to building up camaraderie in an organization, and, two, I did not like being perceived as anything but loyal. I at least thought of myself as more loyal than some of the RBI officials who leaked out information for a small ego boost.

Here is an illustration. Soon after I joined the RBI, a union leader came to me. He was an officer of the Bank. He asked me to plant stories in the media about the management's attitude towards the unions. I told him I would not do it as that was not my job. I also told him that, for internal disputes, the Bank would have some mechanism and he should use that rather than wash dirty linen in public. He didn't like my response.

He told me that the union worked towards the betterment of employees, and, at some stage, I, too, would be a beneficiary of the work done by the union—say, when wage settlement would take place. He asked me if I would refuse the hike in my salary which would be achieved through the negotiation process. I remember telling him that if it was in my purview, I would refuse. Of course, that conversation was futile but it was enough for me to lose faith in the unions and I never became its member.

The grudge would also get reflected in work situations. The RBI recruitment process involved a medical examination. I was also sent to the RBI's medical officer. I was a bit thin and underweight at that time. One look at me and he scornfully said, 'You? You are the new officer for whom a flat in the Bank House has been kept vacant?' Bank House was one of the properties located in a prime locality in South Mumbai where the senior officials of the Bank were given accommodation. It was very close to the RBI office in Fort area in Mumbai. A tiny girl occupying a huge flat in a prime locality was somehow not acceptable to that mindset. In any case, I was underweight, so he quickly put me on a six-month medical probation. After six months, he extended the probation period as I had not put on any weight. I remember telling him to get one of his healthiest officers to work with me and see who could work longer. He, of course, would not listen. One day, Venkitaramanan casually asked me if my job appointment was confirmed. I told him about my medical probation. One phone call from him and my probation was changed to confirmation.

The same was the story of me getting an accommodation. As a senior officer, I was entitled to one. That was a perk and one of the considerations in my joining the Bank—in fact, the biggest perk that the RBI employees get. Like all other government departments and public sector undertakings, the RBI owns properties situated in some of the best localities bought at very low prices in its early days. Since they were built in those days, the rooms of the apartments were huge with high ceilings. Again, one day the governor asked me casually if I had got the house. I said no. He called up someone in the organization and spoke to him, and then asked me to go and meet him. He was the chief of the administration department. As soon as I entered his room, that officer told me that as a senior officer, I was entitled to a house. A house had also been reserved for me. Moreover, I was a lady officer and was often required to stay late in the office and that made my case even stronger. Then he said, 'But I have decided not to give it to you and so you will not get it.' There was nothing more left to say or hear. I was too shocked to react. So, I left his room.

I didn't report this to the governor for obvious reasons. Incidentally, the officer and I came to be on very good terms over the years. I had high regard for him, as he was a good officer who did his job well.

Only a year later, when a new building was ready at Nepean Sea Road—again a posh locality in South Mumbai—was a flat allotted to me. This was a new property, but all senior officers refused to move in because it was farther from the other two properties located in Churchgate and Colaba. And so, it was offered to grade 'Ds' who were the lowest rung in the senior management cadre. But we all lapped it up. The 15-storey building was located on a small hillock and gave a fantastic view of the sea nearby and greenery around. It was well-lit and airy. I fell in love with it at first sight. All the officers who were allocated a flat in this building were young. We would all travel to office together in a double-decker BEST bus. It didn't bother us that, along with us, in the bus queue stood only drivers, cooks and other household staff of the multimillionaires who were the original residents of this area. This also built a kind of camaraderie among us, the young officers, and we began calling each other by our first names, something that was not common in a hierarchical institution like the RBI.

Bringing about a Change

On the work front, I began with asking for a computer for myself. I was used to it as a journalist. Thanks to Tarapore who supported it thoroughly, the first computer arrived in my division. I got it installed in my secretary's room and told him to use it. I told everyone in the division to use it and taught them whatever I knew about it. This was double revolution. First, the Press Relations Division was among the first functions to obtain a computer, when computers in the RBI were rare to begin with, and two, I had it placed in my secretary's room. It was a practice in the RBI to install a computer only in the senior officer's cabin and keep it under lock and key. The officers would hardly use them but, since they were kept under lock and key, others could not use them either. Luckily, my secretary was enthusiastic about learning the operation of a computer and made full use of it. He, in fact, became quite an expert.

There was another colleague in the clerical grade whose job was to count the envelopes in which the two periodicals—the fortnightly *RBI Newsletter* and the monthly *Credit Information Review*, as it was known then—were mailed. These were in the thousands, and I was aghast to see a human being counting them physically every fortnight. When I handed over this job to the printing press which printed those two journals, he came running to me, asking me, somewhat angrily, now that the press was to do his job, what would he do? I told him to learn operating the computer till I found him another task in the Division. Later, he ended up becoming kind of an expert in computer operation, when after a few years he got his transfer out of the Division. Another young peon tried his hand at it too and learnt to type on it. He later took his promotion to become a clerk—that was something!

As computers started taking over the staff's mechanical jobs, they felt insecure. What would they do if machines did their work, was the question that worried them. But before they knew it, new work had been created for them. There was enough talent in those 15–20 staff members in the Division. And getting the freedom to do the task they were assigned, in the way they thought best, made them feel responsible and happy. That was the first step towards changing the small world around me.

Professionalizing the Function

The staff of the communication function was drawn from the general pool of employees in the RBI. They ran the routine functions quite well, but for professional work, I had no one to bank upon. I guess that was why I was recruited and that was the task I took upon myself. I grabbed most of the opportunities that came my way to communicate with the world outside and let the function evolve slowly, rather than following a big-bang approach.

However, communication, to be effective, has to be quick and has to reflect the view of the chief of the institution. I never gave up that privilege of having direct access to the governor, even at the cost of others' envy and wrath. From this perspective, some things were done absolutely right in the RBI.

The Press Relations Division had existed for more than

two decades. It always had a journalist as its head. There were two gentlemen before me who had occupied the post and had shaped the early communication of the RBI in their time. I was the third journalist to be appointed as the head of the Press Relations Division. Well, at that time, press was a major stakeholder for the Bank. With no Internet or website, the only way the central banks communicated with the outside world was through the medium of press. And press it was—no electronic media—as there weren't any televisions or many wire agencies.

The Press Relations Division in the RBI was a part of what is called the Secretary's Department. The department looked after the secretarial function, that is, it served the board of directors of the RBI of which the governor was the head. In that sense, placing the communication function under this department was the right decision. Albeit, that did not give me any access to information. For that, I had to struggle separately.

Yes, the RBI functions like a body corporate. It has a board of directors; some very distinguished people have sat on the board and guided the affairs of the RBI, such as Ratan Tata, Dr A.P.J. Abdul Kalam, Narayana Murthy, Azim Premji, Elaben Bhatt... The RBI governor is the chief executive of the institution and reports to the Central Board of Directors, as it is known. The RBI is also different from a body corporate since the deliverables for the RBI are policy matters—be it monetary policy or bank supervision or management of foreign exchange reserves or management of government debt. In these, the RBI and its governor are quite independent. That is, in the making of the monetary policy or to take over a bank, prior approval of the board is not required. The board discusses only broad issues and gives overall guidance to the Bank's management.

The other right thing to happen was that the RBI hierarchy hardly interfered in my professional work. In fact, my reporting was structured as such to facilitate this. Functionally, I would report directly to the governor and/or the concerned deputy governor, and only for administrative requirements, like my leave, did I need to go through the hierarchy of the department. This more or less left me completely free to design the communication function, as the governor/deputy governors were preoccupied most of the time with their policy matters. It could also be so, because no one, except the governor and the deputy governors, thought that the function was important and required to be paid attention to. And, to some extent, no one had any idea about what exactly needed to be done.

All this suited me well. But it was challenging. At times, I did feel suffocated for not having someone to consult or bounce my ideas off. I would do that with some trusted journalist friends—more in the capacity of friends than journalists, and they would be helpful and honest in their advice. Seeking advice from where it was available and having an open mind proved to be big assets for me. Both helped the communication function take shape in the RBI.

When Venkitaramanan was giving charge to C. Rangarajan, the next governor, he acknowledged my efforts and conveyed the same to his successor. Such were the recognitions that came my way during my entire career in the RBI. Each and every governor appreciated my work in some way or the other. I also got promoted every five to six years, except towards the end when they refused to even consider me for promotion, saying my work conditions did not allow for it. I did not complain or quarrel about it, as promotion was never a priority for me, and getting and having to work with the brightest minds was in itself my biggest recognition.

2

C. Rangarajan

Reforms Set In

Dr Chakravarthi Rangarajan or C. Rangarajan (in office: 1992–1997) is a monetary economist. Obviously his primary interest lay in the making of monetary policy. Having already spent 10 years in the RBI as a deputy governor, he was familiar with the system as well as people and knew his way around the institution. He did not meddle much with other functions and touched upon them only inasmuch as they were required to be for reforming the monetary policy area. There could not have been a better choice than Rangarajan as Venkitaramanan's successor.

There were several reasons. One, having escaped the 1991 BOP crisis by a whisker, India was on the verge of beginning its decade of reforms—reforms that would change the economic face of the country and the way business was being done in India. Since the reforms were primarily aimed at changing the economic scenario of the country, who better than Rangarajan to lead them from the central bank? As a monetary economist, he understood well the importance of simultaneously undertaking reforms in economic, trade, fiscal and monetary areas. Both Rangarajan and Manmohan Singh were economist-thinkers and made an ideal combination for the reforms journey that India was to undertake.

The second reason, and no less important, was that after the unnecessarily controversial tenure of Venkitaramanan, Rangarajan brought in the calm and the focus that were needed to do some real central banking business.

The RBI has always been lucky in having the right governor each time. Maybe the government was, after all, not that villainous when it came to the central bank of the country.

Forming a Solid Team

Rangarajan, ably assisted by Tarapore as the deputy governor at the RBI, and Manmohan Singh, Shankar Acharya and Montek Singh as the finance minister, the chief economic advisor and the finance secretary, respectively, at the finance ministry, formed a solid team that guided the country through economic reforms which put the country firmly on the path to liberalization in the aftermath of the BOP crisis. The Indian economy would change drastically from here on! Never before had anyone thought of a growth rate beyond 3.5–4 per cent for the Indian economy. This was known as the Hindu rate of growth, a term coined by the well-known economist Dr Raj Krishna. The target now was 8–10 per cent.

Changing Slowly

At the RBI, we were still dealing with the Harshad Mehta crisis. Rangarajan, being an economist by training, did not like the journalistic expression 'scam'. The RBI called it 'securities irregularities'. By taking away the word 'scam' from it, we succeeded somewhat in driving the media away from it.

I was barely a year old in the RBI and was still finding my feet. Communication in the RBI at that time meant sending publications to the media, issuing an occasional press release and running two periodicals—one monthly that covered the circulars issued by the RBI and was sent to all bank branches; and the other, a fortnightly that covered news from within the RBI and was sent to all employees.

Although I had prepared a strategy, putting my vision of what was needed to be done on the communication front on the paper, and submitted it to Tarapore for approval, it never came out approved. Much of my journey through the next 26 years in the RBI was on the lines suggested in that paper. From being limited to mere press relations, the division kept adding new dimensions of communication to its fold. Nearly two decades later, from a division it had become a full-fledged department, even bifurcating into curating a museum for the Bank. It was a result of several things: of sheer hard work, of never losing an opportunity to take on any task that even vaguely fell in the communication area and of proving the utility of the communication function in every way possible.

I remember, in August 1996, the RBI put its first foot on the Internet. It was one of the first central banks to have a website of its own. Starting with the annual report of that year, the website was given on a platter to the Press Relations Division. I was not sure if it was a conscious decision of the Bank to let the communication function handle the website or if it was just that the economics department did not want to take up this additional work and that is why the website landed in the lap of the communication function. Central banks have different models—some have their website managed by the technology department, while in others, the communication department manages it. Some have even placed it under the library, as I got to learn later in one of the seminars for central bank communicators!

Hard Work It Was!

As far as I am concerned, giving the website to the communication function was, perhaps, once again, the best decision the RBI took towards better communication. It helped me make forays into other areas of communication and also reach out to other departments. Circulars issued to banks were by far the most important communication between the RBI and the banks. As a journalist I knew that getting a circular issued by the RBI made a news story with a byline. I also knew that it took a long time for any RBI instruction to reach the branch level. Since the instructions via circulars also impacted bank customers, I thought they should be hosted on the RBI website. Initially, I had to persuade the departments to give me the circulars issued by them. It was hard work, as I had to convince them that, first, it would be useful for the public to have direct access to RBI information and, second, by placing the circulars on the website, we would make them available to banks and their branches instantaneously. I would argue that it was the fastest way to reach bank branches and bank customers, who were the ultimate beneficiaries of that information. This would help the customers demand their rights, and banks would have to improve their customer service. Convincing them was a long shot but departments did start giving us their circulars for placing them on the website, and slowly we started building it up from there.

Over the years, I understood the technology bit by bit and used it to build an information base for the RBI. Hyperlinking, for instance, allowed us to make even historical information accessible on the website. With time and technology, the website grew into becoming a portal to access all the information going out of the Bank. Once it became huge, it brought its own problems. Searching for some specific information, for instance, became difficult. Since tools like search engine optimization (SEO) were not available at that time, I had to keep pleading with people, such as the Bank employees and journalists, to use the search option on the website. But who had that much patience? Yet, over the years, the website did become the first point of reference for accessing any information and data coming out of the Bank. Later, we started using it even as a feedback mechanism—a first among the central banks of the world, perhaps. We would place reports and instructions in draft form on the website and seek feedback from all the stakeholders before finalizing them. This helped with compliance from banks. But more on that later.

Learning News Dissemination

We also started announcing the credit policy—as it was known at that time—at a press conference. Credit policy, or monetary policy as it is known now, is the policy through which the RBI announces, among other things, changes in interest rates. On the morning of the announcement, bank chairpersons would arrive to listen to the governor announcing the measures. This would be followed by some discussion. In the afternoon, the media would come. The wire agencies, especially the foreign ones, such as Reuters and Dow Jones, had just started covering India. Wire agencies specialize in covering the news almost as soon as it happens—'flashing the news' as they call it. They compete stiffly among themselves. The reporter who would be even two seconds late in flashing the news that was market-moving or emanating from the central bank would be called in by the agency to explain the delay.

Unknown to us, some media persons, especially from the wire agencies, would wait near the petrol pump right outside the RBI's central office's main gate. As the bankers would step out of the RBI premises, reporters would beg the bankers for their copies of the policy document. Not many bankers would oblige, as the policy document was important for them too. The bankers would go to their offices and get it analysed for business projections and comments for the media. The RBI at that time was rather stingy about giving away more copies, as it was supposedly a secret document till it was published.

This struggle between the bankers and the media apparently went on for a couple of policy announcements. Till, suddenly, on one occasion, a tall reporter from a foreign news agency snatched the document from one banker's hands and ran. Obviously, he won the race by miles by filing the story first. The other reporters were quick to tell me this story, perhaps hoping we would take some action against that journalist. I learnt my first valuable lesson in electronic news reporting. As the central bank of the country, we must distribute the news equitably.

After this experience, we started distributing the policy document to the media as soon as the bankers' meeting would get over. This was done manually, and required elaborate logistics to make it possible. First, the copies of some 20–30 pages were made—initially on stencil printing machines and later on photostat machines. Then, a couple of staff members from the Press Relations Division would carry the copies of the document for the media waiting outside the compound. It was a race against time, as we needed to make many copies, and the portable photocopy machine just could not cope. That's when we made a case for a large photocopy machine called Risograph which could make copies like a printing machine. How I got to know about this machine and managed to get the approval to buy one, even I do not remember today. I guess, keeping my eyes and ears open and asking questions proved to be of great help in recognizing and meeting the requirements of the media.

Communicating Policy Changes

Initially, the credit policy used to be known as the 'credit policy for slack season' and 'credit policy for busy season'. Rangarajan and Tarapore's team was very clear about the concept, which is why these names were changed later. However, I am not sure the media initially understood this change.

In India, the financial year for banks used to be (and still is) from April to March. India was still an agriculture economy and therefore was heavily dependent on monsoons. The trend was that, during monsoon season, between June and September, everyone would observe how monsoons were progressing and how well the sowing phase was being accomplished. Manufacturing activity was dependent upon agriculture. And so, from April to September, virtually no productive activity would be taken up. Which meant that there would be very little demand for fresh credit. The activity would pick up slowly from October and would go on till March, which was the end of the financial year. Since April–September credit was slack, it was called the slack season policy. And, since credit picked up from October, October–March policy was called the busy season policy. It was, however, still the *credit* policy as credit was predominant in it.

As reforms started getting underway, manufacturing and services activities slowly started overtaking agriculture. Slack season and busy season, which were primarily related to agriculture, started sounding irrelevant. Seasons also were slowly starting to merge. So we started calling it 'credit policy for the first half' and 'credit policy for the second half' of the financial year. The interest rates were slowly moving towards being market-determined. The RBI started taking measures to develop financial markets, such as the government securities market, money market, foreign exchange market, and so on. These measures started getting included in the credit policy, which now also had announcements other than just credit-related updates, such as those relating to banking, financial markets and foreign exchange. The credit policy was slowly changing its face and getting broader. It now covered all matters relating to money. So, a few policies later, we termed it the monetary policy.

The monetary policy for a particular year would be announced in April of that year. This would be after the budget was announced, in which the government, in consultation with the RBI, would announce estimates of fiscal deficit (the gap between government's revenue and expenditure) and growth (as gross domestic product or GDP) for the ensuing year. The RBI would then estimate how much money would be required to be supplied to the economy (technically called money supply, the RBI being the creator of money) to achieve the growth projected by the government while keeping inflation under check. The policy measures would then be updated in October once the effects of monsoons were fully known. That, in a nutshell, was monetary policy simplified for the media.

Operating CRR

Rangarajan was a monetarist. For monetarists, money was the protagonist in the monetary policy. The main objective of the policy was to control inflation and this was aimed to be achieved by increasing or decreasing the flow of money in the system. This technically was known as controlling money supply or M3. The main instruments through which money supply was managed were cash reserve ratio and statutory liquidity ratio. Since cash reserve ratio could impact the money supply directly and instantaneously, the RBI, more often than not, used this tool to control money supply. In any case, the RBI did not have the other tools in its kitty at that time. Rangarajan was therefore jokingly referred to as 'CRR' among financial market players. CRR, which is actually an acronym for 'cash reserve ratio', also happened to be his initials!

Tarapore would often privately narrate to me the story of how the credit policy used to be announced earlier. It was literally 'announced to bankers', he would tell me. The governor would chair the meeting with bankers. Only he and the deputy governor in charge of the policy would each have a copy of the credit policy in their hands. After announcing the policy, the governor would ask the bankers if it was acceptable to them. If they agreed, then someone would run and quickly take copies of that document which was kept ready on a stencil. Yes, we used stencils, and the policy was manually typed. If there was a change in the policy, there would be chaos behind the scenes as the entire page would have to be retyped on a fresh stencil and then copied. The copies would then be distributed to bankers present at the meeting, who would then carry it to their banks for implementation. And what was contained in the policy? The policy consisted of a laundry list of the types of loans, how much loan banks were required to give to which category of borrowers and the interest rate at which these were supposed to be given.

Those were the days of what was called 'credit control'—distributing scarce resources to the sectors that were identified as 'priority' or 'preferred' sectors by the government. From those days to today, when a monetary policy committee meets for three days and just announces the changes in the repo and/ or reverse repo rates—the rates at which the RBI lends to and borrows money from banks—it has been a long journey, a journey of almost a quarter century. Somewhere, it has also been the journey of the evolving communication function in the RBI.

Learnings over Tea

Rangarajan and Tarapore, both being monetarists, focussed on reforming the monetary policy area. Rangarajan was a man of few words and believed in hierarchy. Tarapore was quite savvy with the media. He used to often meet media representatives. As a journalist, I once used to be one of his regular visitors. I owe my understanding of the monetary policy and money markets entirely to him. He would call me at around 6–6.30 in the evening. At times, some colleague of mine from *Business India*, where I worked, would join me at these meetings, which would be held in Tarapore's office. Whenever we would visit him, we would be treated to tea served the English way—on a tray, in a kettle, with milk and sugar served separately. And yes, a plate of Bourbon biscuits. It was only after I joined the RBI that his secretary told me that I was among the very few journalists who sought meetings with him. More importantly, I was the only one among those few journalists for whom he ordered the Bourbons! And tea he would serve to us himself. It was a ritual and he followed it to the T.

We would chat for several hours—some market talk, some gossip. This practice continued even after I joined the RBI. He would call me and chat with me often. As a journalist, I could freely talk to him; but after joining the Bank, I became rather conscious and started to politely decline his offer of tea and take his leave as soon as I was finished discussing work with him. Once, he admonished me for this and told me in his typical bass voice, 'Never say no when a deputy governor asks you to have tea with him.' After that, I stopped declining. Obviously. Nonetheless, every sitting with him was a learning experience—either about markets or the way the RBI functioned or even human behaviour, for that matter.

Around this time, I also pleaded with him to allow me to sit in committee meetings. He specifically permitted me to attend committee meetings involving outsiders. Then, on his own, one day, he asked me to attend the meeting of bankers in which monetary policy was being announced. I was to also be part of the press conference announcing the monetary policy. And yes, other colleagues looked at this with envy, making me aware that it was some kind of privilege granted only to me.

I would generally be an observer at these meetings. This immensely enhanced my understanding of the subject, helping me articulate the issue before the media. I was able to respond to media queries effectively, and that gave the media confidence that they could get someone from the RBI to explain what was happening. Misinformation or disinformation got reduced, as I could confirm, deny or give the right perspective to what the media would get out of other members of the committees. That is where, perhaps, the hypothesis of giving communication a seat at the table must have started taking shape in my mind.

As I started attending such meetings, I noticed that the seating arrangement was identical in all meetings. Around a large oval-shaped table, the RBI officials sat on one side and the invited officials from banks, financial institutions and research organizations, as the case may be, sat on the opposite side, both sides facing each other. The chairman of the committee from the Bank's side—usually the governor—sat on a chair with a high back, and the leader on the guests' side sat right across but on a normal chair. Initially, I thought the high chair was meant for the governor but I later realized that it was meant for the Chair of the meeting, even if they happened to be an outsider. The rest of the officials on both sides sat according to hierarchy, flanking the chairman or the leader of the meeting on both sides.

Normally, tea, cashews and biscuits would be served at all the meetings. I observed that, funnily, tea-boys, who really were middle-aged men, would bring tea in the room. The liveried tea-boys even tried to emulate five-star service by wearing gloves! They would head straight to the Chair of the meeting who, normally, would be the governor or a high-level RBI official.

The tea-boys would serve the entire row of RBI officials and then start serving the opposite side comprising the invited high-level banker guests. By the time the tea reached the guests, the RBI side would have finished drinking theirs! This was strange for someone like me who had come from the world of journalism where everyone was treated equally.

One day, when I got a chance to chat with Tarapore, I mentioned this irony to him, that the guests were being served last and the hosts first. The deputy governor understood but could not laugh at it as it was a system which he had been part of for more than 30–35 years. He told me with a straight face and a baritone voice, 'Change it if you can.' I scooted to the in-house chef and broke the good news. The chef, Brian Pais, was a professional and was happy at this news. He told me that he, too, considered the practice to be embarrassing but could not get out of this age-old norm. He had been working at the RBI longer than I had and must have been apprehensive about introducing the change, that too in the governor's meetings.

From the next meeting, he, carefully and without upsetting the apple cart, deployed two tea-boys—one to start service on the RBI side and the other on the bankers' side. This practice continues till date, even though the menu has changed over time. First, biscuits got replaced by cookies, and samosas and pastries got added, which normally no one touched, except some young journalists in press conferences. Gradually, diet consciousness replaced cashews with almonds and dry figs, and samosas and pastries vanished from the plates. I wonder what is served today!

Later, governors, some of whom had worked in the West, and some who were younger, found the high chair for themselves strange and got rid of it. While these changes may appear cosmetic in nature, for me they were indicative of the changing mindset of a traditional organization.

Rupee Convertibility

Reforms were also being introduced on the foreign exchange front. A two-stage devaluation of the rupee was announced through a press release. It was a major event. With the experience of two and a half decades behind me, today I would have done it in a press conference and documented it well. But in the nineties, I was still trying to understand the RBI and the work it was doing. At the time, it was also about following instructions. True, I had an advantage in being a journalist who had covered banking, finance and the RBI and as such I understood the subject quite well. But I was still not an expert in either communication or the RBI functions. So, I simply issued the press release that was handed over to me announcing the two-stage devaluation of the rupee. The press release was quite staid and merely stated the facts in the typical RBI way. It, in fact, did not use anywhere the words 'rupee convertibility'; and expectedly so, as it was just the first step towards freeing the exchange rate.

To operationalize both these reforms—moving towards a market-determined exchange rate of the rupee and gradually moving the rupee towards convertibility—robust financial markets were required. We simultaneously started introducing measures to open up money, government securities and foreign exchange markets too. We needed to explain in detail the way these reforms would operate so that the markets understood what the RBI was trying to do. We needed the media to be our interlocutor in this, as, at that time, that was the only route available to the RBI to reach out. The media was still sharply focussed on Harshad Mehta. Not that we had put the scam behind us; we were still in the thick of interrogation being done by the JPC on securities irregularities. It was noteworthy that, amidst all this, RBI's move towards transparency began at this time itself.

Freeing Monetary Policy from Fiscal Dominance

At the macro level, the government had undertaken economic reforms. These included reforms in the fiscal and trade areas. These were supported by monetary and financial sector reforms undertaken by the RBI. Reforms in the fiscal area and reforms in the monetary policy area had to be undertaken simultaneously. Those were the days of automatic monetization. Tarapore would tell me with a chuckle that it was a clerk who decided when to monetize the government's deficits.

The Reserve Bank of India Act, 1934, ensured that once the balances in the government account went below ₹50 crore, the Bank would automatically issue what were called the 'ad hoc treasury bills' on itself and replenish the government account with cash. The replenishment needed no approval of any higher authority, and even a clerk could issue those bills once the balances went below the threshold level because it was part of a statute. It was therefore called 'automatic monetization'—printing of money as it is known in central bank jargon. This was the route through which the monetary policy remained a hostage to fiscal policy. No one even noticed the volume of ad hoc treasury bills issued by the RBI on itself, which by the mid-nineties were to the tune of a few lakh crores of rupees. Yes, indeed! On top of that were the government securities through which the government borrowed from the RBI. And that is how the fiscal policy or the government treasury dominated the monetary policy. As a large part of money got sucked out by the government to fill its fiscal deficit, very little remained for the private sector. And so the price they paid was much higher than they would pay otherwise, while the government got cheap money—at 4.5% through the ad hoc treasury bills.

This had to stop. And that became one of the first actions on reforms—signing a memorandum of understanding (MoU) with the government to abolish ad hoc treasury bills and stop automatic monetization. This was perhaps the biggest reform in the area of central banking, but was done with no fanfare. The MoU was a middle path, as amending the Reserve Bank of India Act was a parliamentary process and would have taken at least a couple of years. Along with stopping automatic monetization of the fiscal deficit, the government also had to commit to restrain its fiscal deficit—that too not voluntarily but statutorily so that no matter which political party ruled the country, fiscal deficit would remain under check. This again required the passing of the Fiscal Responsibility and Budget Management Act in the Parliament. Convincing politicians to vote for these changes, too, would have been an uphill task. All factors considered, an MoU must have been thought of as a mid-path.

The twin-reform virtually freed monetary policy from fiscal predominance. Once automatic monetization was stopped, the government securities market, too, had to undergo drastic changes. The main reform in this area was that instead of securities being sold at pre-determined interest rates to banks, which were forced to buy them, now they would be gradually moved towards market-determined rates of interest. To achieve this, it was decided to auction the government securities.

Being Media-Friendly

We placed the entire MoU with the government on abolishing automatic monetization of the fiscal deficit along with a press release on the RBI's website. At Tarapore's insistence, we also called a couple of journalists to informally explain the move in detail to them so that they could write and explain it to their readers. It was an informal briefing with these journalists whom we had picked very carefully—we needed journalists who were mature and did not merely chase catchy headlines, those who would understand what we were trying to convey and would write about it on their own, serving our purpose without quoting us. This was important. Tarapore wanted to explain to them the intricacies of the reform but he was completely averse to personal publicity and always kept me in the picture. Luckily, we found a couple of journalists who fit the bill and we worked with them. In hindsight, I think, the approach we had at that time towards the press was the right one. I, too, imbibed a valuable lesson in central bank communication—explain but do not seek personal publicity. This principle I followed throughout. Never did I allow the media to quote me by name or print my photo. But for explanation and understanding, they could approach me any time. This unwritten guideline helped me in the RBI as well as in the media.

Rare Bad Blood

Once, a journalist wanted to interview Tarapore. I did not know the journalist but I was not too pleased about the fact that he spoke condescendingly to me over the phone while asking for an appointment. I mentioned this to the deputy governor and suggested we avoid giving him the interview. He, however, decided to go ahead with it. The interview mainly focussed on the relationship between the government and the RBI with regard to the fiscal–monetary aspect. Those were not the times when the government and the RBI fought with each other in the media. There were disagreements between the Bank and the government but they were not acrimonious and never spilled out in the public domain. The tone of Tarapore's responses reflected exactly this sentiment. However, the story in the newspaper the next day was a shocker. The journalist wrote exactly the opposite of what Tarapore had said. It showed the relationship between the RBI and the government in a poor light. It put both Tarapore and Rangarajan in a very embarrassing position vis-à-vis the government.

The relationship between the government and the RBI had been cordial at that time, barring that longish paragraph criticizing the government on fiscal profligacy that was a part of the RBI's annual report year after year. What differed was only the tone of it. Sometimes it was mild and sometimes harsh. But it was all between two covers. Flashing it across through an interview in a newspaper was new to the Bank. Tarapore had to call the authorities in the finance ministry and explain his position; this left a bad taste in his mouth. Thankfully, the authorities in the ministry knew Tarapore and Rangarajan rather well. And so, with an explanation, the matter was closed, unlike later times when the battles would be publicly fought.

From a communication point of view, this was the first time that bad blood had been created between the media and the RBI. We blacklisted the journalist and barred him from entering the Bank. We even circulated a secret communication among all the top executives cautioning them against the journalist. Even though I was not sure it would work, I did not see the journalist again in the RBI premises for a long time.

Speeches—One More Way to Communicate

Giving a speech to explain RBI's stance on an issue or explaining a new concept to the public was also a method that was used at that time. The media and the economists looked forward to Rangarajan's speeches. He would give one seminal speech and then use the ideas from that speech in some form in other speeches at other smaller occasions. This helped, as the messages were well understood because of repetition. The speeches used to be erudite and comprehensive, which is why journalists would find them somewhat difficult to comprehend. Thankfully, the governor would always prepare the text in advance. Earlier, when we did not have a website, we used to give rolled copies of the speech to the organizers for distribution among the audience. Even then, quickly preparing a news report for the next day's edition based on an erudite speech would be difficult for the journalists.

Tarapore, too, would give speeches which contained a lot of research. Once, I suggested to him that we do a press release from his speech and distribute it among the press along with the full text of the speech. He agreed, despite having some reservations. But when he saw one press release I had prepared, his reservations were gone and he quickly took to it. The idea worked well and we spent a good amount of time drafting the press release. Both Rangarajan and Tarapore were very particular about the expressions they used. Yet, when I would do the press release, Tarapore would often borrow some expressions from my press release to replace his technical writing. I also started accompanying Tarapore whenever he was making a speech in Mumbai. I think he drew comfort in my being around, and the media felt reassured that they would get a copy of the speech from me without any hassle as soon as it was read out.

Communicating Research

Interestingly, what worked with top executives did not work down below. The RBI regularly produces some fine research work. Almost one-third of its staff is engaged in research work—economic research and data analysis. There are several publications of the RBI in which this research gets published. Some publications are periodical and some are occasional. Earlier, there was no fixed time table for publishing them, though. Even the periodical ones would get published as and when ready. With my getting on board, we started doing a media-friendly press release summarizing the research so that it would also be accessible to people with no research background. The press release would be published along with the research paper.

The idea of a press release accompanying the research document got easily accepted, but the research department would end up writing the press release in the same technical language as the research itself. This destroyed the very purpose of a press release. Therefore, I once attempted to rework one. This document was as dense as the research paper itself. As I was no economist, I had to work hard on it to understand the concepts myself before I could summarize them in simple language.

I did it over two days with the help of the economist who had originally written the paper. He was kind and patient, and explained even the most basic concepts to me. Later, when I had gathered some knowledge of economics, I realized just how basic these concepts were and how asking about them only exposed my ignorance. But ignorance, they say, is bliss. And so I unabashedly asked, learnt and reworked. I sent the press release back to the head of the RBI's research department requesting him to approve it. He did look at it and returned it without changing a word. I was wondering whether he had seen the press release at all before returning it with his approval, or had he just returned it, unseen.

The suspense was soon dispelled. I received a call from the head of the research department on the intercom. 'You've done a good job. But I will not relook at it every time. In future, please do not change the press releases coming from my department,' he curtly told me and put the phone down. My attempt at making research accessible to the public had got aborted. I did not reattempt it, until several years later when Rakesh Mohan, the deputy governor in charge of research as well as communication, reluctantly asked me one day to polish a BOP press release. That incident turned out to be quite dramatic.

The release on BOP would get published every quarter. It was sheer comparative data and made for a dull reading. The procedure required approval of the deputy governor on the press release before it came to me for publishing. This time the press release was going up and down the hierarchy with me watching it from the sidelines. While this was going on, I happened to go to Mohan's room for some other work. He was reading the balance of payments press release for the nth time and was clearly unhappy. As I entered the room, he gave me the press release and asked me wryly if I could do something with it. This was a complex subject so I sought some time and took it to my office. When I read it, I felt like rewriting the entire release by putting it on its head. I went back to Mohan to ask him if I could do so. To my surprise, he agreed. I accepted the challenge and went back to my office. Next morning, I went back to his room with my version of the press release. A glance at it and he said, 'This is exactly what I was looking for.'

After that, I worked on the press release a bit more and embellished it with charts and graphs alongside paragraphs. The press release now looked much better and, for a few years, was issued in the same manner. Unfortunately, however, instead of becoming a role model for all research-related releases, the new format was quietly buried and data releases continue to be issued in a drab manner.

Of course, later, when Reddy became the deputy governor, we brought in some amount of regularity in publishing research and data. It was Subir Gokarn who, as the deputy governor, took it up as his agenda to make an outreach to publicize the research done in the RBI. Social media was nowhere in sight at that time. So we kept working on simplifying the press releases.

Economics vs Rajbhasha

In Rangarajan's time, I also witnessed a sad moment. Rangarajan was an intellectual, and no one questioned his credibility as an economist. He could eloquently answer just any question on monetary economics. But when it came to speaking Hindi, he would just fumble. Once during his tenure, a parliamentary committee on *rajbhasha* or official language visited the RBI. Usually, S.P. Talwar and Jagdish Capoor, both deputy governors at that time, being familiar with Hindi, attended to this committee. But this time, perhaps knowing his weakness, the parliamentary committee on rajbhasha insisted that, by protocol, only the governor should receive them and address them. Further, being a committee on rajbhasha, they insisted that the governor should address them in Hindi. And here Rangarajan was clean bowled.

Rangarajan had perhaps jotted a few lines of Hindi before, written in the Roman script, to read out. But a full-fledged speech in Hindi? No way! He tried to explain and excuse himself but the committee was in no mood to give in. And the meeting came to a standstill. It kind of became an ego issue for the committee.

Thankfully, it was soon lunchtime. As usual, we fed the committee our usual good lunch. Over lunch, deputy governors managed to convince the chairman of the committee to allow Capoor to chair the post-lunch meeting. The issue was resolved but the incident buried its feet in my mind. Wasn't Rangarajan appointed as the RBI governor on the basis of his knowledge of monetary economics? Should he have been humiliated this way for not knowing Hindi?

Hindi was an issue with all the governors hailing from the south of India. Reddy used to get away by cracking jokes, and Subbarao would write Hindi words in English script and read them, often making funny mistakes. But he had the ability to laugh it off. Yet, I wonder why Hindi was so important. Language is for communication. By fixing mechanical targets to learn one language and submitting reports on whether those targets were achieved or not, can the language actually be learned? More importantly, can the knowledge of the language be retained? It was this approach that has made Hindi a burden on the public sector. The organizations meet those targets any which way, and sincere learning is given a mere lip service—a colossal waste of resources in the name of what is called the official language, in my opinion.

Gradualism

The RBI never did anything in a big-bang way. Gradualism or doing things by stealth was the way of life. This strategy had its advantages. Changes brought in this way never became an eyesore or hurt any stakeholders. It gave enough time to all the stakeholders to adjust to the change, making it non-destabilizing. Going back, if needed, was easy, as it required minimum change. But, sometime later, as I grew familiar with the institution and my area of function, I started wondering if that was the right way to go about reforms.

In the case of gradual reforms, the changes often became patchy and lost their impact. The stakeholders for whom they were meant never felt the impact of the change and so never appreciated what was done to make their lives simpler. Most importantly, the new rules often overwrote the old rules, leaving behind remnants of the old ones. Such reforms also did not take into account people's mindsets, which often required a complete overhaul. But does that mean that, instead of the gradual change, the big-bang change was the right way to do things? I am not sure.

3

Bimal Jalan

Changing the Institution's Psyche

When Dr Bimal Jalan was announced as the governor of the RBI (1997–2003), everyone was taken by surprise. Jalan had left active administrative services and was in the Planning Commission for some time by then. It was for the first time that a rested official had been called upon to serve as an RBI governor. Be that as it may, coming from the civil services gave a huge advantage to Jalan. Most of the bureaucrats at the finance ministry had either worked with him or were junior to him in the service and would, therefore, listen to him. The governors who had not worked with bureaucrats, and who were too young to command their loyalty and subservience, had to lose out in battle. There was this incident soon after Jalan took over as the governor. Someone in the ministry spoke out of turn on a subject that was in the RBI's domain. Jalan just picked up the phone and spoke to the finance minister himself. Whatever he must have told the minister, speaking out of turn did not happen again during his tenure.

The day Jalan took over as the governor was quite a dramatic one. I was slowly learning the ropes of communication. Media wanted to capture the first few moments of the changing of guard at the RBI. With Jalan's consent, we had arranged a good media presence to witness him taking over the reins of the RBI. Maybe because it was for the first time that we had arranged it or because slowly the media was getting interested in the affairs of the RBI, there was a large media turnout to cover the event.

The RBI's new building in Fort area of Mumbai has a very long ramp in between the compound gate and the entry to the actual building. There was such a flood of cameras—still as well as video—that there would have been a stampede to capture Jalan's entry had we not controlled the crowd with a barricade. While we were all waiting for the governor to arrive, a photographer suggested to me that if Jalan walked the entire ramp, all the photographers who had lined up would get an opportunity to click pictures without any hurry and commotion. I quite liked the idea but was apprehensive about how Jalan would react. I was told he was quite media-shy. So I requested his executive assistant to check this with him. The executive assistant confirmed to me that Jalan had agreed to walk the ramp. Jalan naturally did not know what he was getting into when he agreed to walk the ramp. Anyway, he had agreed, so we—the security staff and I—lined up all the camerapersons at the opposite end of the gate. We sent a message to him that he would have to get down from the car outside the gate where he would be received by the deputy governors and the secretary to the RBI. And then, they all would walk the entire ramp together so that the media would get enough footage and pictures of the new incumbent and his entire team. After this, Rangarajan, the outgoing governor, was to receive him in his room.

Someone must have told Jalan about the media line-up. Media-shy as he was, he reportedly asked his executive assistant if there was a back gate to the Bank from where he could enter. When I heard this, I almost had a heart attack! After raising the media expectations so much, if he were to enter from the back gate, the media would be greatly disappointed and I would not know how to manage them. I naturally told the executive assistant that the new governor could not back out now. I was assured that he would walk the ramp. And he did!

What a sight it was! Everything worked out as planned and Jalan received such a warm welcome from the Mumbai media. For the first time in the history of the RBI was such a coverage arranged. The media also got to capture the moments when the two governors, one outgoing and the other incoming, greeted each other in the governor's chamber—a great photo opportunity for them and a small moment of pride for me. That was the trick! By tweaking the existing practice slightly, I could achieve a lot for the media.

As I was ushering the media out of the governor's chamber after the photo opportunity, I overheard the departing governor, Rangarajan, telling his successor that media relations was in good hands. Such cherished comments from the governors were my biggest reward in the RBI. Apart from such words, I never got any medal or any appreciation letter as reward for my work.

Media-Shy to Media-Savvy

We did a lot of work in the area of communication during Jalan's time. He came in as a shy governor wanting to shun all media. By the time he left, he was a media-savvy governor who had used media very effectively to communicate at various levels. The tracking of the governor's movements and ambushing him to get a sound bite started during his tenure. Towards the end of his career in the RBI, he would be followed and ambushed by the media so much that he had to keep some words and phrases, such as 'no change [in the interest rates]', handy, which he could say without fearing miscommunication. And the media, having got their headline, would immediately leave him to attend to his business.

But this became a vicious cycle. The media followed him because he was sure to give a comment. If he would stop commenting, media would stop following him. But he felt that it would be too impolite not to say anything to them, especially because they used to wait on the streets, rain or sunshine, for the governor to come out of a meeting. I told him, after consulting the media, that it was not necessary to oblige them every time; he could just smile, say hello and move past them, or that he could say something to them only if he wanted to convey something to the market.

Jalan, who wanted to enter from the back door when he had joined, eventually became so savvy with the media that he even started using them to test the waters on some policy issues. He would often get some new thought planted in the media, either through his office or through me, just to gauge how the market would react to it. And I would have to tell the media whom to attribute such news to, depending on how much authenticity we wanted to give to the leaked story. So, the media and I decided on some phrases, such as, 'sources', 'sources close to the central bank', 'sources who did not want to be identified', 'bankers', 'bankers who are in the know', etc., for attribution. The markets were quick to understand the meaning of each attribution. Some were used internationally and some were our own creation. The media took on the role of being the ally of the RBI. Generally, they did not breach our trust; nor did they distort the information that the central bank shared with them. That is how we could gauge the impact of what we wanted to do. For the central bank, this was the first time that it was using media. Fortunately, nothing went wrong; except once, when a minor mishap occurred.

Normally, whenever such news was shared by the governor's office, I would be kept in the loop. Unlike this time. The governor's office shared something directly with a wire agency and the agency published it. The market moved, and I started getting calls from other agencies. Since I was not looped in, I started denying the news, though not on record. A few minutes later, the agency which had got the lead called me up to tell me that the governor's office was the source. I quickly checked with the governor's office and things fell in place. The episode only showed that, if used wisely, the media can play a positive role in central bank communication. In Jalan's tenure, we used media constructively to get market feedback, and it proved helpful.

Explaining the Stance

It was in Jalan's time that we started speaking informally to editors as a group to share RBI's insights and thoughts. We carefully selected the editors who could attend these meetings only by invitation. The meetings were held over lunch. The editors'—who looked forward to these meetings which were held almost once every month—only grievance was that the conversation was so important and interesting that they could hardly enjoy the meal. It was the governor, most of the time, who would tell me to call the meeting. But at times, the media, too, used to ask me to arrange one. And the agenda would be set informally each time. There was a time when the governor even called me back from a small vacation I was on in a close-by hill station. Being the fair and generous person that he was, he sent me a flight ticket and also let the official car remain with my family, who hoped that I would finish work and return to be with them. I could not go back to my vacation, as after the lunch meeting there were follow-ups to be done. But no complaints.

It was at one such meeting that we discussed the issue of converting financial institutions into universal banks. Three major financial institutions, ICICI, IDBI and IFCI, had a severe bad-loans problem, known as non-performing assets (NPAs) in banking jargon. Their inability to raise capital was only worsening the problem. With reforms setting in, the easy options, such as the RBI or the government infusing funds or extending a line of credit at cheap interest rates, were slowly being withdrawn. These institutions were so used to getting doles from the government or the RBI that they never thought of raising funds directly from the capital market even if they were permitted to do so. As a result, the only option left for the RBI was to convert them into universal banks. This would open up the tap of continuously flowing cheap funds for them through savings bank accounts. People generally deposit all their money in savings bank accounts before they invest it long-term. But most forget to carry out their investment plan once the money has been deposited in the bank. Interest rates on savings bank accounts are usually the lowest. Thus, savings bank accounts give access to cheap funds. I remember clearly, a well-known economist editor from a financial paper asked the governor about who was going to give long-term finance to industry after financial institutions became banks. I don't remember how he replied. Perhaps, he mumbled something. But the question was real. The problem of lending long-term from short-term funds created a mismatch between sources and usage of funds, but this would hit these institutions hard only some years later.

It was in another such meeting that the governor dropped a bombshell. In his inimitable style, he laughingly said to the editors, 'Once you get back to your office from this lunch, Alpana will announce a rate cut.' Everybody looked at me as if I knew something about it. My jaw had dropped hearing this. If any editor present there were to leak this out or write a story on that before any formal press release, the market would immediately react. Thankfully no one did that. Perhaps they did not take him seriously. Neither did I. Would any central banker do such a thing knowingly? But this was Jalan, we all forgot. He could do anything. And sure enough, by 3.00 p.m., as the markets were drawing to a close, I had the press release announcing a cut in the interest rate in my hand. Later, while remembering this event, all of us in the media would laugh heartily.

Unfortunately, the discussions at these meetings slowly degenerated. As word got out that the governor regularly met media persons, two things happened. First, the market started listening closely to these meetings—though these were off-the-record meetings and the media could not write about them, they briefed the markets informally. The media persons, though bound to secrecy, gave a peek into these meetings to the markets over telephone conversations. This was not so much of a problem for us. Second, editors started nominating beat reporters or seeking invitations for multiple people from their organizations. Each time there would be a request, I would check with the governor. I would also give him a little brief on the journalist's mindset but he would invariably agree to the new entry. The governor—in fact, not only Jalan but even other governors—would never say no when I would approach him with a request for the inclusion of an editor. So, the lunch table became larger and larger. At one such meeting, Jalan even remarked that he would now have to get a microphone to speak to them.

This inability to say no to journalists sometimes created unpleasant situations. Once, a journalist with a peculiar nature sought an invitation to the meeting. The governor asked me to invite this person against my advice, which we did. But a few meetings later, we had to drop this person out due to their misinformed and misdirected reporting against the government and the Bank.

Another instance was peculiar too. There was this leading financial newspaper that once wrote a baseless and slanderous news report on one of the deputy governors. We slapped a legal notice on the newspaper and against the journalist who wrote the news report. A few days later, we held our usual luncheon meeting with the governor. My natural reaction was to debar the financial newspaper against which we had issued a legal notice. But when I asked the governor if we should invite them, he said yes without batting an eyelid. For once I argued, saying we had just taken action against the paper. But he said that it didn't matter. A valuable lesson was learnt. Never let ego come in the way of your work.

This also created another problem. Whenever requests to let an additional person from the same organization attend the meeting would come, I would first offer to replace the existing attendee with the new one. This would, for a meeting or two, put them on the back foot, as no one would like to give up the privilege to attend the governor's meetings. We also had a genuine reason for restricting the number of media persons to such meetings. First, it was no press conference that anyone could walk into it, since we did not expect or want any reporting of these meetings. The objective was to only explain issues so that they had a clear understanding and RBI's point of view was reflected in their reporting. Two, the larger the gathering, the lesser the control over reporting for the Bank. When we selected the original participants, it was based on the knowledge that they would not breach our trust. But when editors sought entry for their colleagues, it was based on who covered the beat. There was no 'selection' and so there was no control. Some editors asked and got the reporter's entry cleared from the Bank, introducing them as a replacement while others wanted an additional entry. The number of participants increased and became unwieldy for a closed-door chat.

With a larger number of media persons present, I had to tell the governor to be a little circumspect while talking, who naturally started holding back. This meant that slowly the talks stopped being as insightful as before. This became a vicious cycle. Since conversations were not insightful, editors stopped attending and sent their beat reporters instead. The reporters, who came to the meetings looking for a headline, perhaps did not understand the significance of these meetings and were therefore not mindful of the protocol and rules of the game. And one day, my fears came true. One mid-level journalist covering banking wrote a news story about what was discussed at the meeting. Gradually, others also started doing the same, sometimes getting their colleagues to write the story so that technically they would not have breached protocol. The meetings had to be called off.

That is the difference between an editor's point of view and that of a reporter's. It is not a question of juniors and seniors, but editors generally do not crave for a byline and would rather get a peek into the central bank's mind. For a reporter, bylines are a ladder to promotions and better prospects. So they are always tempted to write whatever they can lay their hands on that will give them a byline. Another noteworthy point in this is that central banks are never headline-hungry. They would rather not be in the headline. But most journalists do not appreciate this. They would push their ground-level reporters to attend these meetings on the pretext that they reported on the central bank. What the editors could have done was to attend the meetings themselves and brief the reporters on what was discussed or how the central bank thought.

In another incident, an editor of another financial newspaper sought permission for an additional journalist's entry. I deliberately did not revert to him. My presumption was he would come alone. To my surprise, he did not turn up; he instead sent his beat reporter for the meeting. I expressed my astonishment at the junior reporter's arrival loud enough for others to hear, so that even others knew that he was not invited. Other journalists and perhaps the reporter must have thought that I would ask him to leave. For them, I wielded power. They also knew I was somewhat strict in such matters. But knowing the governor's approach in such matters, I knew I could not have asked him to leave. I left it at that. Here was the thin end of the wedge. Should I have asked the journalist to leave? Would the governor have supported my decision? It would have undoubtedly established my control over press matters in the eyes of the journalists present there. But I preferred to maintain good relations with the media. I think it ultimately paid off, as throughout my tenure in the RBI, we managed to keep the media on our side.

Being Resourceful

One day, Jalan called me to his room early in the morning and said, 'I want to convey this message to the market. Can you suggest a way?' He did not want a press release, only an oral communication so that the market would correct its behaviour. I thought for a moment and asked him if he was speaking at a public forum anytime soon. As luck would have it, he was addressing an industry forum that afternoon itself. So I told him to keep the sentence that he wanted to announce with him. I told him that I would get a couple of journalists to ask a pointed question and he could say the sentence that he wanted to convey to the market. He liked the idea and agreed to play along. The drama played out successfully, adding another trick up our sleeves.

After that we frequently used this trick. After he spoke to the media on the sidelines, we would issue a press release saying, 'On the sidelines of…the governor told the media…' This was for those media persons who missed the sideline comment and also for the markets. There were also times when we would just issue a press release which opened with a 'On a query from the media, Jalan said…' Often, the 'query from the media' would be a made-up situation and the sideline comments became a powerful communication tool for the markets. For the media, it became a new job—to track the central bank officials for sideline comments. Successive governors and deputy governors faced this and made good use of the opportunity. The attention it gave them was formidable. To avoid unequal opportunity, we also started publishing their public movements on the website. This was a move towards greater transparency. Although, as a communication strategist, I sometimes did not like the central bank playing to the media's tune.

Correcting the Media Reports

Jalan, like all other governors, was very sensitive to what appeared about him and the RBI in the media. He would want to correct even a small error in reporting. We must have perhaps issued the maximum number of letters to editors in Jalan's time for such corrections. He would also himself write and send to editors small handwritten notes marking the corrections in news reports. While we pointed out the mistakes, we also wrote in our communication that this was for their understanding and not for publication. This would save them the embarrassment while getting the correct information and understanding for the future. If we were not to do this, we would perhaps have become a nuisance to the media, which would have been receiving a corrigendum letter from the RBI almost every day!

Jalan used to be quite upset initially when, with every small movement in the rupee's exchange rate, the media would declare a 'record rise' or 'record fall', using similar expressions for rise in foreign exchange reserves which had started building up in his time. Every week, when we would publish the data, the media would say 'record rise' even if the rise was as small as a 100 million dollars a week in this context. Jalan would often joke about this with the editors at luncheon meetings.

Another trend which evolved during his time was forecasting the value of the rupee. The media would report market estimates based on the real effective exchange rate (REER) and nominal effective exchange rate (NEER) every time the exchange rate moved. NEER is the current exchange rate as you and I would know it—the price of the foreign currency in rupee terms. For instance, if the exchange rate of the dollar is ₹85, the NEER of the dollar is ₹85. NEER adjusted for inflation is the REER of a currency. Jalan did not like the media forecasting the value of the rupee based on these metrics. He would explain his dislike by saying that it became a self-fulfilling prophecy, as the market tried to achieve the forecast. And to bring back the rupee to its fair value, the RBI had to resort to intervention, and that cost the country money. But media being media, they never learnt to use these expressions correctly. Although, they did bring technical concepts like REER and NEER into focus.

The Change

Jalan was a very unorthodox governor. He would often wear a bush-shirt, trousers and sandals to office and walk into meetings with bankers all suited-booted. He would come in by 9.30 a.m. and walk out of office at 5.45 p.m. sharp at the end of the workday. Unlike a bureaucrat who gloated about the pile of files lying on his table, there were no files left on his desk when he left every day. He did not want the files being simply pushed upwards in the hierarchy without any value-addition. Much of level-jumping or not adhering to hierarchy protocols came into the RBI during his time.

His way of functioning, too, was non-traditional. He would travel to Delhi almost every week. We learnt later that every week he would go and meet various parliamentarians—not only those from the ruling party but also from opposition—to create favourable opinion towards policies among them. Most of the public relations professionals would say that relationships are built in peace times and used in war times. He actually practised it—a lesson that all leaders should learn. Discussions on relevant issues happened beforehand and behind the doors so that when the actual decisions were announced, there would be consensus. Most of the time outsiders did not even know about the role Jalan or the RBI played in resolving a crisis. Splitting UTI into two institutions after the Harshad Mehta scam, raising the barriers ahead of Pokhran II to protect the country from foreign exchange outflows that might have occurred in the aftermath of Pokhran-II or the Asian crisis were cases in point.

Freedom to Speak

This one happened in the midst of the Asian crisis. By this time India had opened up significantly in the trade area, easing foreign exchange flows. To prevent the flight of foreign exchange from the country, India did not hesitate to reverse some of the measures taken to liberalize the flow of foreign exchange. The world criticized India for this but it did not deter Jalan, who had Reddy as his deputy governor. A crisis team was to constantly be on the vigil to see unusual movements in the foreign exchange market. Banks' foreign exchange exposures were watched on a continuous basis and statements were used as a major communication tool to manage the sentiment of the market.

On one particular day, movement in the foreign exchange market was quite unusual and a statement had already been issued to calm the market. At the end of the day, we also kept a statement ready with the intention of releasing it the next day a little before 9 a.m., so that the markets would read the statement as soon as they opened for trading and would be guided by it.

Just like the other members of the team, I, too, kept a tab on the market. The next day, at around 8.45 a.m., I spoke to a couple of journalists to find out how the market sentiment was. The market, I found out, was calm with normal activities. So, I felt that issuing the statement would create unnecessary ripples in an otherwise calm market. In fact, issuing the statement would have shown the nervousness of the central bank, causing the market to react to it in a negative way. I called up the leader of the crisis team, who was also the head of the department that looked after foreign exchange reserves and the RBI's intervention in foreign exchange market. The leader also agreed with me that there was no need to issue the calmative statement we had prepared the previous day. Now the question was who would bell the cat? Who would tell the governor that his decision need not be implemented! The mantle fell on me—the youngest and the junior-most officer in the team.

It was well known that Jalan did not like to be challenged. He was used to his orders being carried out and not questioned. Well-wishers had warned me when his name was announced to be the next RBI governor, 'Follow the orders. Do not argue with him.' Not that I was argumentative, but, at times, I did insist on getting my viewpoint across. So when I was told to call up the governor and tell him that the statement was not necessary, I naturally hesitated.

By this time it was already 9 a.m. I had no choice but to call. The first question the governor asked me was, 'So? Has the statement been issued? What is the reaction of the market?'

I sheepishly informed the governor that the statement had not been issued and the overall view of the team was to not issue it, as it could prove to be counterproductive.

There was a moment's silence at the other end. And then, the governor said, 'Oh… Fine, then… Don't issue it now. Let's meet in the office at 11 a.m.' With that, the phone disconnected.

Recalling the advice that I was given when his name was announced as the governor, that he would expect his instruction to be carried out, I feared nothing less than the loss of my job. Yet, when I went at 11 a.m. to the governor's room, to my surprise, the entire crisis team was present, the mood was light and the governor was laughing. On seeing me, he said, 'Good job! You have saved us from embarrassment,' or some such thing.

I realized that he actually appreciated my not carrying out his instruction in the interest of the Bank. The freedom to put forth one's view, even if one were the junior-most and even after the decision was made, always existed in the RBI. But this episode gave me the confidence to express my views without fear, and I went on doing so unhesitatingly.

Off the Record

When the Ketan Parekh scam (2001) spilled out in public domain, it was quickly brandished as a co-operative bank scam—obviously so, as it had reared its ugly head in one very large co-operative bank in Gujarat, the Madhavpura Mercantile Co-operative Bank (MMCB). It was true that co-operative banks were the epicentre of the scam. But it was also equally true that the RBI had spotted it. MMCB was borrowing heavily in the money market for several days, and that alerted the RBI to get into investigative mode. It was found that the bank was being abused by a stockbroker.

The moment the scam spilled out in public domain, an urgent meeting was called on the eighteenth floor, where the RBI governor's office is located. I clearly remember Governor Jalan, the deputy governors, the executive director in charge of co-operative banks and myself in the meeting, along with some other people. There was a discussion about the course of action. When it came to the topic of media, everyone looked at me. I was clear about some things and I clearly put those across. The first of these was that there was only one spokesperson to whom all media was directed and that spokesperson should be me, not only because I was the appointed one but also because, in the RBI, I was one step away from the real scene of action and so less vulnerable while answering media queries. Everyone quickly agreed to this.

Then, hesitatingly, I made another suggestion regarding the line of conversation with the media, of telling them facts which would put the blame clearly at the doorstep of the government. I also said that I would single-handedly deal with it; that if anything went wrong, I would take the blame for it; and that the management should, in such an eventuality, not stand by me. In effect, I was putting my job at stake. The only condition was to keep me briefed on developments at all points in time.

For years together, the RBI had been recommending action against the corrupt management of co-operative banks in its annual inspection reports to the registrars of co-operative banks at the state level. It had also been making long-term recommendations to the Centre to clean up the co-operative banks. But for the politicians, co-operative banks were the metaphorical milch cow that none of them was willing to give up. And so, the malpractices continued in this sector.

As expected, there was pin-drop silence for a moment, and then the governor very firmly quashed my second suggestion down. 'No, we will not blame the government,' he said. The meeting ended.

Everyone stepped out of the governor's room. I, being the junior-most, was the last one to leave. In those days, the deputy governors also had their offices on the eighteenth floor. The floor had four deputy governors' offices, lined one after the other, after which was the office of the governor. As people dispersed into the corridor, they entered their respective rooms one by one. Towards the end came the office of the deputy governor in charge of banking regulation. As he was entering his office, he turned his head very slightly and told me to come in with him. His gesture was so faint that I could have missed it. The others went ahead, and I entered his room. Once inside, he plainly asked me what else would I need for my plan to be put into action. I was taken aback but did not show it. I just reiterated what I had said in the meeting about needing to be kept in the loop all the time. He said, 'Okay, go ahead.'

I did not know what I was getting into, but what started after this moment was a one-(wo)man war against the authorities. No one spoke to the media except me. I was part of every meeting that was held to discuss the matter. And, over and above, the deputy governor in charge of banking regulation (sometimes even the other deputy governors) and the executive director in charge of co-operative banks kept me briefed on all the developments every day. I was on top of the situation at any point in time. I remember speaking to the media all day long in my office. Most of the time, when the media would say that they had found something new, I had to refute their claim, because whatever they had 'found', the RBI had already found and reported to the government—central or state, as the case may be—but no action had been taken, thus implying that the government was to be blamed (without really blaming it directly) and not the RBI, effectively killing these stories every single time. Since the media could not write against the RBI enough, they gradually started referring to it as a stock market scam.

I had no doubt in the media strategy that I had suggested or in my capability of handling things. What I till date have not been able to figure out is, how could the deputy governor, who otherwise was quite gentle and docile, take the bold step of going against the governor's order? Was he so scared of losing his job or his reputation that he decided on his own to go with what I had suggested? Also, at some point in time the governor must have guessed what was going on. Why did he not do anything to stop it, especially when it was against his order? Did the deputy governor take the governor's consent subsequently? Or did the governor turn a blind eye to what was happening because it suited everyone?

Whatever may be the case, the crisis did blow over, and I was happy to have played my part successfully. Whether anyone recognized it or not, whether I would go down in history or not—who was bothered about such things at that time?

The point is: media is hungry for stories, and if you don't feed them yourself, they might cook these up on their own. Feed them right and, if convinced, they will certainly be on your side. Gone are the days when one could get journalists to write whatever one wanted merely by taking them out for drinks and lunch or dinner. Most of the media houses today pay better than before and have strict codes of conduct. Today, if the journalists meet their sources in restaurants, they are expected by their employers to pay for whatever they eat and drink. In this case, all my talking happened in my office. I never took any journalist out and still most of them wrote in favour of the RBI, convinced as they were about the RBI's work. Also, keeping the spokesperson briefed helped. Getting the responses right across the phone or through a personal visit made the journalists call the spokesperson first rather than go all over the Bank in search of answers and getting a scoop in the bargain.

In the Rightful Place

In many ways, Jalan's tenure as the governor was the best for RBI. Not only did the employees gain their rightful status among the banking fraternity but even the Bank got its rightful place vis-à-vis the government. Governor Jalan made sure that the RBI governor had the final say in choosing who he would work with—his deputy governors, his board of directors and even bank chairpersons. We had some of the most highly coveted people on the RBI board during his tenure. Over the years we have had on-board the likes of A.P.J. Abdul Kalam, former principal scientific advisor to the government of India; Y.H. Malegam, chartered accountant, senior partner, B.E. Billimoria & Co. Ltd.; K. Madhava Rao, state election commissioner, Andhra Pradesh; Mihir Rakshit, director, Monetary Research Project, ICRA (formerly Investment Information and Credit Agency of India Limited), Kolkata; K.P. Singh, chairman, DLF group; D.S. Brar, CEO and MD, Ranbaxy Laboratories; N.R. Narayana Murthy, chairman and CEO, Infosys Technologies; A.S. Ganguly, chairman, ICI Ltd.; H.P. Ranina, advocate, Supreme Court of India; Elaben Bhatt, chairperson of SEWA Bank; and V.S. Vyas, economist and former director, Institute of Development Studies, Jaipur. Each of them was a stalwart in his or her field.

Jalan also ensured that the RBI governor chaired the selection committee for bank chairpersons and deputy governors, and had a major say in choosing his successor. In fact, it was Jalan who had chosen his own successor. Reddy, who had left the RBI for IMF only a year ago, was called back to take over from him as governor. Jalan convinced the government that he was the only worthy candidate for governorship. He also insisted that Reddy came with a straight five-year tenure.

This had never been done before. All appointments were made initially for three years and then were given extensions for two years and a further two years. Jalan believed that this didn't serve the purpose, as three years were too short a period for the governors to plan their tasks. The talk in the corridor at that time added a bit of masala. It was being said that, for Reddy, the change would come at a huge personal financial loss, as from earning a tax-free salary of thousands of dollars, he was being called for a job that would offer a salary of a few thousand rupees! Moreover, he would have to forego the advance rent he had paid for his apartment in Washington, DC. Well...the rent part I am not sure of, but the salary part definitely holds water. Even if all the needs of a governor were taken care of by the RBI, purely in monetary terms one would earn less.

Pre-emptive Communication

Jalan had taken to media like fish to water. He knew how to manage various stakeholders and was very result-oriented in a subtle way. The RBI had undertaken a significant step during his time with the mechanization of the currency area, which was predominantly in the hands of the unions. We had ordered currency verification and processing systems. At that time we had a huge backlog of soiled currency notes, which were piling up due to the agreement with the unions restricting the output of employees. We needed machines to take care of the huge backlog and the future requirements of note destruction.

Unions over the years had become quite weak and could not protest much against the mechanization in the RBI. But they also knew that if the RBI succeeded in its effort, they would lose their very existence, not only in the RBI but also in the banking industry. The union leaders were old and well-respected by both employees and bank managements. One could not find any fault with them; they were impeccable in their knowledge of the subject they handled and their work ethics. Given the threat, they sought a meeting with Jalan. The morning of the meeting, the governor called me and asked me to scribble out a few sentences about the meeting with the unions. He gave me the outline. He approved what I had scribbled out and told me to keep it ready as a press release. As I was leaving his room, he said, 'You also attend the meeting and bring along the press release.' So, I went to the meeting with that paper in my hand.

Jalan had the habit of saying something serious with a laugh. The laugh would be quite loud and even appear artificial, but since he was the governor, everyone laughed with him; in all that laughter, the serious message would get conveyed lightly. That day, in the meeting, he welcomed the union leaders with that laughter and an informal hello-hello. Once everyone was seated, he called the meeting to order. Then he said, 'Before we start the meeting, we will share a little press release. I will ask Alpana to read it out. If you agree with it, both parties can say the same thing to the media and our discussion can then be free and frank.'

The unions were taken completely by surprise. The bait of free and frank discussion worked and they immediately agreed with the wordings of the press release, which virtually said nothing about the deliberations at the meeting. Jalan then invited the unions to say what they had come for. The unions were so helpless and disarmed that they could not be forceful or aggressive. They just said that the governor knew what they had come for and requested for the RBI's help in saving their face before their constituents. Jalan again laughed in his typical style and said that he did not know much about it, that the matter was being looked after by the deputy governor (Vepa Kamesam at that time, who had come from the SBI), and that the unions should discuss the matter with him. The unions knew the deputy governor well. He was quiet but tough. They knew that there was no point talking to him; the vibe at the meeting was quite clear. They also understood that the deputy governor would not be able to do anything if the governor was not supporting it. After that, the conversations in the meeting only bounced between weather and tea-biscuits. When I again read the press release while issuing it, its meaning came fully to me. The press release had actually pre-empted an ugly spillover of issues in the media while saving the face of the unions.

Awards and RBI

Inviting the RBI governor to grace an event is quite common. In fact the invitations are so many that if the governors start accepting even half of them, one governor would have to do *just* that—grace events! There are also quite a few awards instituted for banks, some of them by media houses. They would publish a special issue on banking, give 'best bank' awards and feature them in the special issue. It would be a kind of advertorial issue, which would get them good advertising revenue. The awards would be given by some dignitary at a public function. Given the choice, the media houses would not settle for anyone less than the RBI governor. Once, Jalan was invited to hand out banking awards instituted by a financial newspaper. He went to the function and gave away the awards. When he came back from the award function, he told us that he was not comfortable with the idea of the RBI, or its representative, giving away best bank awards. It was too much of a reputational risk, as

RBI had no idea about, and no control over, the process of selecting the best bank. And, someday, this could backfire. He asked us to frame guidelines for the governor about what kind of functions to attend and at whose invitation. I don't think anyone actually worked on this, but after this episode Jalan did not take part in any award functions, restricting himself to accepting invitations only from associations of industries, such as the Indian Banks' Association, Confederation of Indian Industry, Federation of Indian Chambers of Commerce and Industry, and never from any particular industry house or media house. Later, most governors, more or less, followed this unwritten norm.

Rules Took Away What the Law Gave

Jalan and Reddy as a team had worked out their roles quite clearly, or so it seemed. Monetary policy had just been freed from the fiscal dominance; the focus of foreign exchange regulations, too, had shifted from 'control' to 'management'; and the banking sector was learning to breathe freely. New instruments and new institutions were being introduced to develop and nurture the financial markets that would help operationalize monetary policy. Trade reforms required a thorough revision in the legal framework, which was restrictive and needed to be amended to facilitate trade. Even banking business was being deregulated. Yes, deregulation was the buzzword.

It is difficult to explain in just a few words the momentous changes that were sweeping the economy. One incident that occurred at that time may somewhat explain this drastic change. There was a junior officer in what was at that time known as the Exchange Control Department. He was simple-hearted and talkative. Once, I met him in his department, which was a huge hall with tables and chairs for employees laid alongside the windows. The centre of the hall, too, was lined with chairs and tables, but not as neatly. Officers sat at the tables along the windows, while the other staff sat in the centre. At that time, there used to be many questions in the public's mind regarding the momentous changes that were taking place. The questions would reach me through journalists. To be able to explain things to them, I would seek the help of friends like this officer. If I did not understand the rules myself, I would ask them to explain those to me. And then, I would respond to the journalists with a satisfactory and comprehensible answer. One day, this officer, who must have been explaining some rule to me, said, 'Madam, it is very difficult, you see! First, we were sitting on this side [he pointed towards one side of the room] and our job was to find out any strand from the rulebook to *prevent* foreign exchange from going out of the country. Now we sit on this side [he pointed to the opposite side of the room] and our job now is to find any strand in the rules to see if we can *allow* foreign exchange to be sent out.'

I could understand. It required a change in the mindset, which was difficult. We perhaps needed to explain the changes and the philosophy behind these changes to the employees in the government, in the RBI and in the banks. We also needed to explain them to the public. This would have perhaps made the changes go down well with all those for whom they were meant. But no one thought about this. Once, I spoke about it with my counterpart in the government and she just gave me a wide-eyed look. Here, the communication machinery had failed. Reforms still trudged along but they were not accepted wholeheartedly and their impact was not felt as much as it ought to have been.

Let me give one more example. The Jalan–Reddy duo was as if on a liberalizing spree. They were trying to bring in simplicity in foreign exchange rules to ease business transactions. They were also looking at regulations that were making it difficult to remit money abroad for personal use, like, education, medical treatment and other such small expenses. Changes were being introduced in regulations at a fast pace through the Foreign Exchange Management Act (FEMA). But the impact was not being felt on the ground. Complaints were pouring in. This made Jalan and Reddy wonder why the changes were not facilitating ease of business.

One reason was that the staff at the bank branch level did not keep themselves up-to-date with such daily changes. This is true even today. Another, and a more important, reason was interesting. It so happened that, one day, Reddy expressed his lament to me when I had gone to see him for something. I told him what I had once overheard in the Exchange Control Department. The officers were quite worried about the pace with which rules were being relaxed. 'We will lose control,' they feared. The process was, and even today is, that the government frames the regulations under the Act after discussing these with the RBI. This is so because any change in regulations means amending the FEMA. Once the FEMA is amended, under those regulations, the RBI frames the rules. The rules are then circulated among banks, helping them implement those regulations in their business transactions.

What was happening was that, on the one hand, the Act was being amended to loosen control, and on the other, while framing the rules, the RBI officers would bring control back in some manner, causing the relaxations in the regulations to lose their effectiveness. Businesses, therefore, kept complaining. When I told Reddy this, he was shocked—rather, exasperated. He immediately announced the setting up of a committee to 'review' all the rules, not only under foreign exchange but also banking rules. He specifically asked for some young officers to be nominated on this committee, hoping that they would bring in the desired change. He named it the Regulation Review Authority. I am not too sure whether the committee succeeded in the task assigned. After all, the officers who were assigned the task of changing the rules belonged to the same milieu as those who wrote them! The next version of this committee came only in 2021.

Giving Us Our Dues

The RBI officials were, at that time, paid quite poorly. There wasn't much in terms of perks either—no car even for the head of the department. Once, Parameswaran told me that whenever there was a meeting with the bankers at the Indian Banks' Association, and he was invited, he would prolong leaving the premises after the meeting got over simply because the bankers would come in their chauffeur-driven big cars and the head of the department of banking regulation at the Reserve Bank of India did not even have a car! Bankers were kind. They knew this and, therefore, would offer to drop him back to the office. But Parameswaran, just like any other RBI officer, was too self-respecting. So he would wait under some excuse or the other till all the bankers had left, and only after that he would go down, quietly hail a cab and reach his office.

This situation changed remarkably in Jalan's time. He not only ensured that we got a respectable salary but also other necessary perks, including a car with a driver, and, most of all, a liveable home. Like any other public sector undertaking, the RBI provides housing to its staff. Many of these facilities are located in prime areas of state capitals.

They were built many years ago and have the old-world charm with huge rooms, high ceilings and green surroundings. But, from the inside, they looked shabby. Since they were constructed many years ago, they needed maintenance and an upgrade—repairing, painting, inclusion of modern amenities. Even the toilets were old-fashioned with Indian-style squat toilets. Jalan agreed to get this done. Today, the RBI staff lives in stylish but moderate homes.

As for the governor's bungalow and governor's office, Governor Jalan believed in good living. He bought a few art pieces. He had brought with him some of his own artefacts, while buying some more on the RBI's account. He, however, got the department to make an inventory of the art—those which were his own and those which were the RBI's, both at his house and his office. He made sure that, when he left, he took only his own art, and left everything that belonged to the RBI behind.

Giving Up

Jalan decided to give up his third tenure a bit early; he had been given a three-year term to begin with, followed by two terms of two years each. We arranged his exit interviews with the media, and I too pitched in for the interview for our internal four-page periodical. I had started these exit interviews with the top management of the RBI for our internal fortnightly called the *RBI Newsletter*. In fact, these used to be rather free-flowing conversations, as we would already get quite a bit of material on official matters through the interviews conducted by the media. At the end of the exit conversation with Governor Jalan, he, with his inimitable laughter, thanked me. I was naturally embarrassed to hear that and told him humbly that whatever

I had done was part of my job. On hearing my response, his laughter turned into a smile and he softly said, 'No, no. Your being there helped!'

Once again, I felt rewarded.

4

Y.V. Reddy

Master Administrator

Dr Yaga Venugopal or Y.V. Reddy first served as deputy governor (1996–2002) and then as governor (2003–2008) of the RBI. His approach to the two roles was markedly different. 'Earlier, I was the deputy governor and could get away with anything because the final responsibility lay with the governor. Now, I am the governor and the buck stops with me,' he once told me in the context of media interface.

As deputy governor, he had focussed on the development of the financial markets. That was the need at that time, as well-functioning financial markets were necessary to effectively operationalize the evolving monetary policy. They needed to have both breadth and depth. When he took over as the governor, financial markets were fairly developed and were by far efficient. But, somewhere along the line, financial sector reforms had taken a back seat, which he wanted to bring back into focus. As the governor, he had set this as a priority. The banking sector in its entirety—public, private, co-operative and non-banking finance companies—needed to be cleaned up of NPAs and, structurally, in the corporate governance area. That it was going to be an uphill task, we all learnt the hard way—especially Reddy who, as the governor, had to balance both the government and the financial sector.

Right Policies and No PR

Governor Reddy's way of functioning was very different from that of Jalan. But both of them were very effective and unique in their own ways. Jalan was not a man of the masses. On smaller issues, he functioned through his executive assistant who knew his mind well. He was also very practical and, ideologically, always walked the middle path. He was a master of public relations. He would take Delhi in confidence before he started working on any solution.

Reddy was his opposite in many ways. He did not believe in any such niceties. He went ahead with implementing policies that he thought were right for the country's economy. 'If my policies are right, they will speak for themselves,' he told me when I had suggested we try and build a favourable opinion by taking media into confidence before announcing any major changes in policies. This was my first attempt to move the RBI communication to 'lobbying', as it was then known. Now, it has evolved into thought-leadership and is a powerful public relations tool. When I learnt that Reddy would not use lobbying to generate support for his policies, I knew that my effort to reach the next level in public relations might have to wait a while to succeed. In the RBI, it was only me who thought we should lobby to get the right policy accepted. To the world, it did not matter.

Reddy was kind, easily accessible and very affectionate. For him, all men were *paa*s and all women were *maa*s in the typical Andhraite way. By addressing people so, he would endear himself to everyone. Though not as frequently or as easily available to the media as he was when he was the deputy governor, he was still loved by them. He would crack jokes with them and deal even with their frivolous questions with a wisecrack, though in a very friendly and non-offending manner.

Broad-Based Decision Making

There were many initiatives taken during this time. Governor Reddy disrupted almost every function of the RBI and taught us to do them differently. He was consultative. In fact, he had a penchant for setting up committees for consultation. Each monetary policy during his time would see a few committees being set up to review some regulation, some issue. But there was a reason behind that penchant. 'Democracy is good,' he would tell us. 'There is benefit in consultation,' he would explain. This way any opposition not only got expressed but could also be addressed and resolved.

Setting up committees to resolve complex issues had another advantage. This way, different stakeholders were brought to the same table. They would discuss the issues threadbare and also suggest solutions. Once the solutions came from the stakeholders themselves, there was very little for anyone else to disagree with. Everyone got an opportunity to express their views. Discussions took place before the decisions were taken. And once the decision was taken, everyone implemented it.

Reddy also set up many internal committees so that the departments could consult each other on common issues. The RBI was (perhaps *is*, but to a lesser extent) an institution that worked in silos. This lack of coordination, especially in supervisory and monetary policy matters, did not help. Reddy had already started with a financial markets committee when he was the deputy governor. The committee comprised all the departments that had anything to do with monetary policy—the policy, markets, foreign exchange, research and, at times, even supervisory departments. The committee would meet every morning before the markets opened and discuss market conditions and the RBI's strategy for the day. In times of crisis, it would meet even during the day, and as many times as the situation required. The discussions were so useful it soon became one of the most important internal committees at the RBI.

More committees were set up to discuss supervisory issues. Committees across regulatory institutions, such as Securities and Exchange Board of India (SEBI), Insurance Regulatory and Development Authority of India (IRDAI) and others, were also set up by Reddy, which later evolved into the Financial Stability and Development Council (FSDC) headed by the finance minister, with the RBI governor as the alternate chairman. Just like the financial markets committee, Reddy also got the supervisory departments to come together once every week and discuss overlapping supervisory issues. The discussions at this committee were useful but it could somehow never achieve the stature of the financial markets committee. Coordination in supervision could have achieved so much. This was demonstrated only during Rajan's time, when simultaneous inspection of borrower accounts in all the lending banks was undertaken and the true state of non-performing accounts got revealed.

Some committees were permanent, as the issues at hand were such—perpetual. Reddy would call them 'standing committees'. There was one each for the government securities market, foreign exchange markets and, later, money markets, as reforms in these areas were ongoing. There was one for co-operative banks. Then, there were committees which were set up around some specific issue. These committees consulted all stakeholders, produced a report in about three to six months and got disbanded. It was then for the RBI to work further on the suggestions made.

There was a pattern for the two-way consultation. First, a committee would be set up; after which, its report would be placed on the RBI website for feedback. Then, the draft regulations were prepared on the basis of the committee's recommendations and feedback was received on the report. Next, the feedback received on draft regulations would be incorporated in the final guidelines for implementation. At this stage, the opposition would have virtually been nullified.

Media, at times, would make fun of Reddy's enthusiasm for setting up committees. But, somehow, it was working. Many reforms could take place in many areas. Consultation or two-way communication is what he started in a big way, and the Bank's website became an important tool for this.

Once the policy was announced, Reddy would be reluctant to alter it. 'As the governor, I set the goals. I am flexible on the time frame for achieving the goals, but my goals would not change,' he would tell us. At times, he deliberately set a short deadline to achieve the goal. Bankers would obviously make a hue and cry about it. He would then relent and extend the deadline. But bankers could not change the goalposts. That was one smart strategy.

Reforming the Co-operative Sector

Two major focal points for Reddy as the governor were reforming the co-operative banking sector and the non-banking financial companies (NBFC) sector.

As in the case of any other reform, a crisis created an opportunity to bring about a change in the co-operative sector. The MMCB episode, discussed in the last chapter, was that crisis. Ketan Parekh, a stockbroker, had, for many years, been using MMCB and other smaller co-operative banks financially linked with it to finance his stock-market operations. RBI found this out when it observed that a small co-operative bank like MMCB was regularly borrowing huge sums of money in the money market. A quick investigation revealed the broker's misdeeds, and the bank was put under an administrator.

The issue was complex, as many small co-operative banks in Gujarat had kept their money with Madhavpura, and letting Madhavpura fail meant these banks, too, would fail, creating a domino effect on other banks as well. The crisis had actually happened in 2001 when Reddy was the deputy governor. The sector was, however, still not out of the woods when he returned as the governor.

Co-operative legislation in India is about 150 years old. The objective of this legislation is very noble—to encourage thrift, self-help and co-operation among people. That is how co-operative societies came to be established, and many of them, over time, converted themselves into co-operative banks. Co-operations are listed as both central and state subjects under the Indian Constitution. Unfortunately, after being spotted by politicians, this sector became a can of worms.

As discussed earlier, banks are where people place their hard-earned money as deposits in savings bank accounts and earn a small interest, before investing the money for a longer term to earn higher interest. In reality, what happens is that, instead of keeping the money for a short duration in a savings bank account and quickly investing it in long-term assets, people often neglect or forget to invest it further. In other words, savings bank deposits provide a very stable and cheap source of funds to banks. The banks in turn lend the money to those who need it and earn interest. This is the reason why banking, including co-operative banking, is a very lucrative business, and anyone who has the means to start a bank wants to have a bank in their portfolio some day or the other.

The financial institutions were converted into banks in the mid-nineties for the same reason. Instead of providing large amounts towards capital to take care of their bad assets, converting them into universal banks ensured a steady and cheap flow of funds through savings bank accounts to them. By making the denominator (deposits) larger than the numerator (bad loans), the percentage of bad assets looked smaller than it really was.

It also created another problem which surfaced some years later—financing long-term assets with short-term liabilities. Financial institutions were typically into project finance, which had a tenure of three to five years or more. This was a big folly, and the banks so created (IDBI Bank is the biggest example, as it could never get out of its legacy of large bad loans) always remained weak; except ICICI Bank, which changed its model and turned itself into a real retail bank. But that is another story.

Apart from the steady flow of money and power, there was another reason why politicians found the co-operative sector very lucrative. The sector was lightly regulated. Most of the co-operative banks, even today, are typically the 'friendly neighbourhood bank', having a single branch or, at the most, a few branches. They were inspected every two or three years, as they were too small to pose a systemic threat, and because RBI does not have the resources to inspect them every year. More importantly, because of the politics intertwined with it, regulating and supervising co-operative banks were difficult tasks for RBI. The sector always fell between two stools—on the one hand, the central and the state governments and, on the other, RBI. Co-operative banks are governed by the banking regulations formulated by the RBI. This is the first conflict area. The governments often prevented RBI from framing regulations that even remotely seemed to take their control over co-operative banks away.

The second area of conflict was supervision. In theory, co-operative banks are supervised by the RBI. But, administratively, they are under the government of the state in which they are headquartered. So, RBI would supervise the bank, find irregularities, recommend action to be taken—most of the time against the board—and wait for the state government to take the action recommended. In fact, first there would be large gaps between the RBI's periodic inspections of these banks, and then there would be huge delays in the follow-up of its inspection findings at the state government level. The follow-up action in many cases would never happen. Corporate governance was—and perhaps is even now—very poor in these banks.

The cost of poor governance is borne by the helpless small depositors who have kept their money—often life savings, worth a few thousands or maybe a few lakhs—'safely' in the bank. To save this small depositor, the RBI often takes the ultimate step of liquidating the bank so that depositors at least get back their deposits through Deposit Insurance and Credit Guarantee Corporation (DICGC). In reality, the process of liquidation is long-drawn and the depositors have to wait for years together to get their money back. Ironically, the management, who is often the culprit, gets to know of the RBI's action much before the depositors through the inspection report that the RBI shares with the management as a part of the supervisory process. Between this report and the action by the state government, the management withdraws all the money it has in the bank, leaving very little for the depositor.

Reforming this sector meant improving both regulation and supervision. Ideally, politics should stay out of this sector. Reddy, a master administrator, knew well that the central and state governments would never give up control over these cash cows. So, he designed a strategy. It was quite clear that any effort to amend the law to divest the governments of their control over these banks would never succeed. To address the issues arising out of dual control, an MoU was designed. This would be signed by each state and the RBI regional office of that state. Under the MoU, a committee called the TAFCUB (Task Force on Co-operative Urban Banks) was to be set up in each state for the co-operative banks in that state. The members of this committee comprised the highest official from the RBI in the state, namely the regional director; an official from the urban co-operative banks department from RBI's central office; the registrar of co-operative societies of the state; and a representative each from the National Federation of Urban Cooperative Banks and Credit Societies (NAFCUB) and the state federation of urban co-operative banks. The objective behind appointing such a high-level committee was to have such members who could take decisions on the spot, rather than have members who would deliberate and suggest, but would have to leave the decisions to be taken by someone else sitting in another office, days, months or years later. Hence, all those who would be involved in the decision-making were made part of the committee.

All the decisions relating to the operations of the urban co-operative banks in a particular state were to be taken by this committee across the table. The committee was empowered to recommend whether the licence of a particularly weak co-operative bank in the state should be withdrawn or not, or whether a licence should be given to a particular group of people to start a new co-operative bank or not. Reddy had insisted that the officials on this committee would be those who had decision-making powers. There was no 'going back to office and taking approvals and reverts'. And that applied to RBI too. This brought the central government and state governments together on one table. In return, the RBI offered to help the co-operative banks of the state that had agreed to sign the MoU through training their human resources and upgradation of technology.

'A small cost to pay,' I still remember the governor telling us in an internal meeting. If by helping the co-operative banks to train their human resources on issues such as corporate governance and technology we were going to help them improve their customer service, and, thus, if they started complying with regulations on their own, then the cost of a few crores hardly meant much. And, thus, RBI began its journey on the reform path for the co-operative banks.

Deputy Governor V. Leeladhar, under Reddy's guidance, personally worked with some of the chief ministers on signing those MoUs. Andhra Pradesh was the first state to sign it.[2] After that, there was virtually a queue of states wanting to sign the MoU. Today, most of the states are under the MoU, and the co-operative banking sector has benefitted quite a bit from this arrangement.

Reforms in the Non-Banking Sector: Reforming NBFCs

NBFCs and residuary non-banking companies (RNBCs) were another lightly regulated sector and therefore open to malpractices. Reddy's contribution to reforming the shadow

---

[2]'Regulating Co-operative Banking', *Reserve Bank of India*, http://tinyurl.com/yckj2bry. Accessed on 2 February 2024.

banking system, known as the non-banking financial sector in India, was phenomenal. That also included reforming the RNBCs.

When Reddy took over as the governor, there were four RNBCs. Two major RNBCs were particularly an eyesore for the RBI. Both these companies—one was based in Kolkata and the other in Lucknow—had a similar model to garner money. They functioned through their agents. Their agent network was extremely well-spread. As agents, they collected deposits from acquaintances and neighbours, friends and family. Since for everyone the 'agent' was a known person, they would not hesitate to entrust their hard-earned money as deposits with the agent. These companies also offered a higher rate of interest. Receipts for the deposits would come later but were many times not issued. They were not on the company's letterhead, not signed by company officials, and at times not even stamped. There were no signboards on branches. But they would have collected thousands of crores of rupees as deposits. What they did with the money was anybody's guess.

At that time, the RBI did regulate them but not too stringently. Regulations existed only on the deposit side, as RBI's main concern—be it banks or NBFCs—was and is protection of depositors' money. By regulation, the RNBCs had to invest most of their deposits in secure assets like government securities and lend only a small amount. But, since the lending side was totally unregulated, that's where these companies made hay.

Both the RNBCs were politically well connected and, therefore, very powerful. The reform in this sector began on a very low pitch. The governor made it clear at a meeting of the four RNBCs that, in the interest of the depositors, the tightening of regulations for RNBCs was inevitable. Two companies clearly got the message and voluntarily agreed to wind up after fully paying off the dues of all the depositors.

An overhaul in the way these companies were to be regulated came initially through small changes. Whenever a fresh amendment in regulations was issued, no one immediately understood the far-reaching implications. The most significant change in the regulations was that 80 per cent of the deposits were now required to be invested in government securities. That left only 20 per cent of the money with the RNBCs to play around with. The effect of this regulation slowly started affecting the RNBCs. Small companies quickly complied. One of the large RNBCs based out of Kolkata, too, started complying, and ultimately stopped accepting deposits from the public, returning all the money taken over time. The other one in Lucknow was still very powerful. It put up a strong resistance to the Bank's new regulations.

The RBI, led by Reddy, was in no way going to relent. His approach, though, was quite reconciliatory. Whenever a request came for discussions, it was favourably considered. Of course, he himself did not hold any meetings with these companies, but the deputy governor in charge of the department regularly held quarterly meetings with the chief executives of the companies for almost two years.

Yet, the matter went to the court, and the court directed the RBI to hear the chief executive out, which the RBI did. And how? The chief executive arrived at the Bank with his entourage, with media in tow. We stopped the media at the gate. Being Mumbai media, they knew the RBI's approach towards them. They obliged us and stopped outside. On the Bank's side, the department that regulated the NBFCs, led by its head, sat through the meeting. The chatter was that the chief of the department was briefed to quietly listen to the chief executive of the RNBC. This was an anti-climax, as everyone who had been following the case would have thought that there would be fireworks between the governor and the chief executive of the RNBC. But what happened was just the opposite. Interestingly, in this entire drama, Reddy and Leeladhar, who was the deputy governor at that time, remained in the background. It was only the department that faced the RNBC, fought the battle peacefully and won! After nearly two days of listening, all the chief executive got was a timetable, spread over a couple of years to comply with the regulations and return all the public deposits that it had collected. A plan to repay the depositors meant for the RNBC closure of its business.

The RBI tightly monitored the company till all the deposits were paid. Sadly, the company was permitted to branch out into mutual funds, insurance and real estate, and it continued to collect money from gullible depositors through those routes. Even though the RBI shared the information with other regulators on a real-time basis, other regulators gave permission to the RNBC to start a mutual fund and an insurance company. Was all the money from the RNBC parked there? I have no idea.

What was surprising in this and many such episodes was that—be it courts or the media—questions were asked only of the regulator and never of the regulated. The media constantly kept asking us questions about the case, what we were doing about the misdoings, and so on. I am not sure if similar questions were asked of the miscreants as to why and how they did what they did. How can you distrust a regulator, which, in other words, implies trusting the regulated? Reddy never told us how he thought of this strategy and how he executed it. Perhaps no one asked him that!

Bank Mergers

Cleaning up the financial sector and its consolidation included closing down some banks too. There were too many small banks in the private sector. The RBI had to take up compulsory mergers of these small banks with larger banks mainly for two reasons. First, globally, the banking regulations were changing with respect to capital adequacy ratios, income recognition norms and some kind of uniformity in the way of identifying NPAs. The small banks started by individuals/family were not able to meet the rigours of these tighter standards, but did not want to give up the control of banks.

Second, as the financial sector started opening up, aspirants who wanted to get into the banking business found these small banks to be sitting ducks. The aspirants were mainly larger banks, foreign investors and fraudsters. They would invest in these banks, initially as per regulations. But their ultimate objective was to take them over and start running their banking business as their own when permitted to do so. This was also the time when banks were being asked to augment their capital. There were some other banks which found it difficult to raise money towards capital, as they belonged to one community and did not want to go out of the community to raise money. This brought some instability in the sector. Having fewer but stronger banks was perhaps more desirable for the Indian financial system. Merger of smaller banks with larger and stronger banks was a good solution.

However, merging banks was not an easy task. The experience of merging two banks—New Bank of India with Punjab National Bank—way back in the nineties had left a bad taste in the mouth. The cultures of both the banks were quite different even though they were both North India-based banks. So, while finding a partner for a weak bank, it was not enough that the stronger bank had adequate capital. The merger also needed to be advantageous to the stronger bank. Organic branch expansion and getting ready-made branches in areas where the stronger bank had none was a gain for the stronger banks. Additionally, by now, banks were also using technology for core banking, that is, the basic banking function had been computerized. If the technology platforms of the two banks were not the same or compatible, then merging them would be difficult, as the technologies would not speak to each other. So, similarity in technology platforms was another condition.

I am not sure whether or not the regulatory department had conducted a study of banks, but when RBI decided on merging one bank with the other, they seemed to be matching quite well. Preference, of course, was given to voluntary mergers. Smaller banks were being coaxed into finding their own partners for merging. Some were forced to merge to save the depositors from losing their hard-earned money. It was a win–win situation for all.

The number of such mergers was not very large. Still, to do it without disrupting the sector was a challenge. The strategy was to announce that the bank had been placed under moratorium on a Saturday afternoon after the close of business, and the bank would reopen on Monday morning in a new avatar—as an entity merged with a stronger bank! The strategy worked so well. There was no run on the bank. The depositor was not inconvenienced at all. And the merger happened over the weekend. The markets wondered how the RBI found and convinced the stronger banks to take over the weak banks. I remember having requested the head of the regulatory department to write down the details of the mergers for posterity.

Finding a Solution

Reddy almost always found a way to strike a balance between the conflicting demands of the government and the banks. Take for instance, the issue of the RBI appointing its own officer as one of the nominee directors in public sector banks. Since the time the RBI started deregulating, it wanted to remove its nominee directors from the banks' boards. It was clearly a conflict of interest as the RBI was also the banks' regulator.

Banks, however, had found an ally in the RBI's nominee directors. They were the only ones who fearlessly opposed any loan proposal that was not creditworthy but was pushed by the government or any other director. So, the banks would run to the government each time the RBI would put forward the proposal to remove its nominee directors from their boards and convince them to prevail over the RBI against its proposal. The government would oblige and the RBI would not be able to implement its proposal. This went on for many years.

When Reddy came in as the governor, he again pushed for removal of the RBI's nominee directors. He nearly succeeded in convincing the government to get them removed. But this was not getting implemented. He, then, found a brilliant solution to this quandary. The government and the banks wanted an RBI official on the banks' boards, but the RBI did not. So, he proposed to have retired RBI officials on banks' boards as the RBI nominees. The government and banks both lapped up the proposal. The nominee was an RBI official alright, but retired, and so the issue of conflict of interest was taken care of! And banks could continue to rely on the RBI official who directly or indirectly protected the banks from unwanted pressures. Even today, the RBI nominee on banks' boards is a retired RBI official.

The First Taste of Technology

Those were the early days of mobile phones. The mobile phone technology gave the RBI a taste of the lightning speed with which communication could take place, and how far and wide. Every April comes a spate of holidays which force banks to remain closed for business for almost a week if combined with Saturday and Sunday. With large-scale ATMs and other modes of electronic payments coming into play, this should not have mattered much. With various lobbies at work, however, this would always get criticized and media would wait for just that one mishap to occur to bash banks up.

It so happened that over one such long weekend, an ATM of a large private sector bank in a city in Gujarat went dry. Refilling ATMs is an outsourced service and is a logistics issue. It is a drill well-orchestrated with the cash vans doing pre-designed rounds of ATMs. The routes are fixed and cannot be changed easily. Those were also the days of bank closures and mergers. So people were a little weary. When the ATM of this bank went dry, message travelled over mobile phones that the private bank was in trouble. And the news immediately became viral. From Gujarat, it reached Chennai and Hyderabad in a matter of two to three hours. There was almost a run on the bank as people queued up in front of its ATMs to withdraw their hard-earned money.

The bank came running to the RBI. The RBI knew that the bank did not have a solvency problem. It was simply a question of the bank's inability to replenish the particular ATM with cash due to holidays. But a run can make even the strongest of banks go bankrupt because banks do not keep all the cash as cash. They lend the money out. And they can lend ten times of the deposits they have collected. Some of their money is also invested in government securities and other bonds as part of the regulatory requirement, such as statutory liquidity ratio (SLR) and CRR.

Knowing that the bank did not have a solvency problem, the RBI agreed to provide cash to the bank. The next issue was that of logistics. Collection of the cash from the RBI's currency chests and its delivery to the branches and ATMs was a huge logistical challenge for the bank. Somehow, this was managed, and the depositors started getting their money back. It was, however, necessary to let the public know that the bank was sound and there was no need to worry.

The bank again requested the RBI to issue a press release assuring people that the bank was sound and they should not panic. This was a dilemma. As a regulator and supervisor of banks, the RBI, in principle, cannot stand behind one bank and call it strong. Next day, another bank could come and ask for the same assurance from the central bank. More importantly, if, today, it stood by a bank and said it was strong and healthy, how many would understand that the statement was contextual? It being sound and strong today does not mean that it will remain sound and strong forever. Moreover, this had happened earlier. A press release issued by the RBI assuring the strength of another private bank did boomerang a few years later when the bank busted and had to be merged with another one.

With great hesitation and circumspection, finally the RBI agreed to issue the press release. The communication department of the bank was in constant touch with me. I told the communication person to ask all the branches to download the press release from the RBI website when issued and display it at their branches and ATMs. I also suggested that the CEO, an assertive speaker, should appear on television and appeal to depositors to not withdraw their money. Those were the days when interest rates were dropping. Not only would a premature withdrawal attract penalty but making fresh deposits would also have to be at a lower rate of interest. The strategy worked and calm returned to the bank after a stormy weekend.

More Initiatives

Reddy also started calling finance secretaries of states to the RBI. He invited the finance secretary of the central government and the chairman of the Planning Commission, as it was known at that time, as well as officials of the tax division of the finance ministry to this meeting. The state finance secretaries found these meetings so useful that the RBI started arranging these meetings every six months. Many of the reforms in state-level finances came as a result of these meetings, as the RBI provided the crutches that the state finance secretaries needed to bring about reform. Over the years, this forum has facilitated key decisions on model fiscal responsibility legislation, revisions in limits on Ways and Means Advances (WMA) and Overdraft (OD) Regulation schemes, adoption of auction method for market borrowings and setting up the Consolidated Sinking Fund and Guarantee Redemption Fund, besides others.

'Open Mouth Operation'

Reddy had given a speech in Goa in 1997 as the deputy governor. The rupee at the time was overvalued, that is, its exchange rate against the dollar was higher than what it should have been, given the performance of India's economy. Intervention from the RBI would not have been without the accompanying costs.

To prevent the rupee from appreciating, the RBI could intervene in the foreign exchange market to suck out the excess foreign exchange. This would generate rupees, as the RBI would buy the foreign exchange at market rate. This meant more rupees in the market. The RBI would again have to intervene in the market to suck out those excess rupees. Conducting these operations would come at a cost. You cannot have the excess foreign exchange sloshing around in the market as that would make the rupee appreciate. Since India is a developing economy and has a higher inflation compared to developed economies like the United States (US), its currency should be depreciating against their currencies. The RBI's buying of foreign exchange would of course swell up the country's foreign exchange reserves, but it also meant immobilizing the foreign exchange that came into the country, as the foreign exchange reserves could not be used even for development. With the RBI buying the foreign exchange from the market, it would give rupees to the selling banks. Having excess rupees would cause inflation. This meant one could not leave the rupees sloshing around in the market either.

So, the RBI thought of an 'open mouth operation'. I was unaware about this strategy. I remember, Deputy Governor Reddy called me to his room late one evening. He gave me a rather longish speech—his speeches were never short—to read. It was difficult to concentrate and read while sitting in front of the deputy governor. One would be conscious of taking their time. Somehow, I managed to read it. When I read the last sentence of the speech, I was taken aback, though I did not show it. He asked me what I thought of the speech. I gave him some general remarks. He then specifically asked me about that last sentence and how, in my view, the market would take it. My answer was unambiguous. I told him that the market would go into a tizzy. He smiled and let me go.

Apparently, in my reaction he was testing waters. What if the market did not take the hint? It was quite a risk to take. But when I expressed that the market would react, it convinced him and other speech writers in the external operations department that they could go ahead with the speech and expect the market to take a hint and correct itself. The market, the next day, did go into a light tizzy, which we later called 'correction', and the operation was known as 'open mouth operation', derived from 'open market operation'. The phrase was coined by Reddy himself, and it meant that the RBI managed to 'correct' market behaviour by not directly intervening in the market through money but by giving it a verbal hint to correct its course. We achieved what we wanted at no cost, compared to what cost we would have incurred had we intervened in the market.

It was only just before leaving the RBI for the IMF—an assignment he had earned—that Reddy called me to his office and asked me if I remembered the Goa speech and what I had told him. I said yes. He laughed and shared with me that it was from my response that they—he and the other speech writers—were assured that the 'open mouth operation' would be successful and decided to go ahead with the speech. I was not sure whether to feel happy or foolish!

Under Fire

One more speech brought him under fire—this time as the governor. If I remember right, it had not even been one month of him having taken over as the RBI governor. The issue was whether or not India should allow foreign investments through participatory notes (P-Notes, as they were popularly known). P-Notes are financial instruments through which foreign investors or hedge funds invest in Indian securities without registering with SEBI. The structure of the instrument would hide the identity of the real investor as one participatory note would have clubbed a few investors. The regulators obviously did not like it. Reddy was dead against allowing them in the country. This was because it was difficult—almost impossible—to identify the ownership and the colour of the money that came in through this route. The government was, however, keen on allowing them because they buoyed the stock markets. It had even set up a committee under Dr Ashok Lahiri, who was the government's chief economic advisor at that time, to examine the issue, and it had given its report, naturally in favour of allowing them to invest in India. Budget announcement was nearing and there were very strong rumours that the government was likely to allow foreign investments through P-Notes in the country. 'How can I allow it?' Reddy said very earnestly. I could see the tinge of sadness that a soldier would have at the battlefront upon knowing that he was fighting a losing battle but still having to fight! It was clear that he would do anything to prevent this from happening.

Reddy wrote a speech. The speech first narrated the recommendation of the Lahiri Committee and gave counterarguments to that in the next paragraph. It was written in such a way that first would come the recommendation of the Lahiri Committee, and the very next paragraph would be his own views, logically demolishing the Committee's recommendation. The RBI governor making a speech just before that year's Budget was a candy for the media that had gathered in abundance at the venue. I was waiting in my office for a signal to upload the speech on the RBI website. Soon, I saw headlines flashing on wire agencies. They began filing headlines as the governor began to speak. And all hell broke loose.

One wire agency reported the first paragraph as the RBI governor's views. As we know, the speech's structure was such that the first paragraph was the verbatim reproduction of the Lahiri Committee's recommendation; Reddy's views were in the following paragraph. This was gross misreporting. In his anxiety to be the first to report, the wire agency's reporter had horribly goofed up.

Typically, on wires, first, the headlines would flash, and soon after, the full paragraph would be published under that headline. The governor's views—that he was against allowing foreign investments through P-Notes—were widely known in the market. Suddenly, when the wire agency reported a headline favourable towards P-Notes, the markets naturally reacted. On reading the flashes, the kerb market went into an absolute tizzy. The stock market was nervous, and the rupee threatened to open very weak the next day.

But this was a smaller mishap. Much later, the reporter who had misreported apologized to me, saying it was his mistake due to which Reddy suffered. The bigger mishap happened when the full intent of the governor's speech was understood. The market commentators went into a tirade against the RBI and its chief.

There was tremendous pressure on Reddy to withdraw his comments and make a statement to the media so that the markets would be calm when they opened the next day. All this drama was taking place after markets had closed for the day. Perhaps the finance minister had already indicated this to the Delhi media. So the television crews had lined up in the foyer of the RBI building in Mumbai to record a statement. I was summoned to give my input on how to manage the crisis. As I reached the governor's executive assistant's office, Reddy had also come out of his room. He told me that he would not want to change a word of the speech, and therefore there was no need to speak to the media. Having said this, he went back to his office. Within no time, he rushed out again into the executive assistant's office and told me that the finance minister had already made a statement in Delhi. It appeared that he had no choice but to give a statement to the media. (Much later, Reddy would tell me that he could withstand the finance minister's insistence but when the prime minister called, how could he say no?)

Suddenly, I could see fatigue on his face, which had coloured up. This happened when he was faced with some task that was against his grain. I suggested that he take the speech copy in his hand and read out the two controversial paragraphs, on which the media had already reported, verbatim into the television cameras. This should make it apparent that it was the media that had misquoted him, that Reddy had not changed a word from the speech given and he stood by whatever he had said. He seemed to have liked the idea. I got all the television cameras which were waiting in the foyer into our conference room and Reddy read out from his speech the two paragraphs—the first one describing the Lahiri Committee's recommendation and the other with his response to it—as I had suggested. Once done, he withdrew into his office, without looking up into the cameras. This was very unlike him. It was clear even to the media that he was not happy doing this. Some even asked me if he did it under pressure. It seemed to have achieved the purpose. The fact that he spoke to the media to 'clarify' gave an impression to the market that he had changed his stance, and that brought calm. The market opened quiet the next day—perhaps because of the finance minister's assurance, but everyone got the impression that Reddy had changed his stance, reassuring the market. At that time, the storm seemed to have passed.

There was a side story that was taking shape while we were recording the statement. As I went back to my room, there were calls waiting for me. By now it was in the open that Reddy's policies were not being received well in the market. Commentators and analysts were on a rampage. Among the many calls I received was also a call from an oft-quoted bank economist. He asked me if I had heard a foreign commentator's criticism of Reddy on a leading business channel. I had not. He told me that the commentator was actually abusing the governor on national television. The economist told me that I should call the owner of the channel and ask him to stop telecasting such abusive commentary. I heard the commentator the next minute on the channel and was aghast. I called up the owner and the business editor and requested them to do something about it. It, however, took quite a while to take the commentator off the channel. Not only that, they also banned the commentator from their channel forever. A few days later, I heard that the commentator had been asked to leave the country by his employer the day right after he had hurled abuses on air.

The channel was otherwise very respectful—of the country's central bank and of its governor. So, the owner, who was based in Delhi, called me up and asked me if he should come to Mumbai and apologize to the governor in person. Knowing Reddy, I told the channel owner that I did not think it was required and that I would still ask the governor and revert to him. I went to the governor's office to ask. Before that, I went and reported this to Leeladhar, the deputy governor, who at that time was temporarily holding charge of my department. He asked me what should be done. I told him that the RBI was too big an institution to be bothered about such abuses. The channel had already taken corrective action and we should just ignore them. He agreed and told me to convey my view to the governor. I went to Reddy. He asked me the same question. What should we do? I said the same thing—just ignore. He agreed completely and wholeheartedly. So I came out and conveyed this to the owner of the channel. We were all relieved, thinking the second storm had passed too. But had it?

I was returning to my office when K.J. Udeshi, another deputy governor who was in charge of administration, called me into her office. 'What are you doing?' She asked me. For a moment I felt out of my element; *what is she asking about*, I wondered. Then, immediately, I realized that she was asking me about what had just happened. So, I told her.

On hearing me, she said, 'No. It's not over. You must write a strong letter to the channel and take some action against them,' she told me.

I told her that the deputy governor in charge of communication and the governor himself had approved of my suggestion of no action. But she insisted.

'I am telling you to do it as the deputy governor in charge of administration,' she told me.

Her argument was that, since it was all about Reddy, he should remain in the background, but we, as an institution, should take it up for him. She was well-meaning, I am sure. But I had settled the matter with the governor. Somehow, though, I got swayed by that argument and wrote a somewhat strongly worded letter approved by Udeshi to the channel.

The owner, being a thorough gentleman, immediately wrote an apology and faxed it to the governor's office. Reddy called me again to his office. 'What is this, maa? We had decided no action…' he told me with anguish clearly written on his face.

I tried to explain, but he was right. I had, for once, not obeyed the order of the head of the institution; rather, I had gone against his order. It was that moment when I could have lost the governor's confidence in me. And had that happened, I would have had no option but to leave the institution. Leaving, by itself, was no big deal for me, but leaving because of losing the institution chief's confidence was not acceptable. Even at that moment, it was clear in my mind that a communication officer could not hold her position if the head of the institution had no confidence in her.

Earlier, before going back to my room from Deputy Governor Udeshi's office, I had casually confided in the governor's executive assistant about Udeshi's order. Somehow, we both missed that we should have sought Reddy's advice on the matter, and he, being a master administrator, would have shown us a way out. But confiding in the executive assistant did help me. The executive assistant, who happened to be in the room when I was summoned by Reddy again, thankfully confirmed my version. Reddy was kind. He forgave me. And I survived.

Corporate Fraud?

There was one more time when I had advised the governor to take the media on his side. A foreign bank which had a very aggressive head wanted to buy a comparatively new Indian private bank which was promoted by a large mutual fund. The banking sector had not yet opened up to foreign investors. Again came into the picture Reddy's conservative policy. He had once explained to us that Singapore's banking sector was fully owned by foreign investors. Its central bank head had once expressed his fears to Reddy, that if, one fine day, the investors decided to withdraw from Singapore, there was nothing he would be able to do! Singapore's banking sector could be held to ransom by foreign institutional investors (FIIs), Reddy had said. He did not want that to happen to India, especially because the banking system kept the poor man's deposits. He was walking towards opening up the banking sector to foreign investors in baby steps.

When this foreign bank wanted to invest a very small percentage in the private sector bank, Reddy asked the then deputy governor in charge of banking regulation to find out if it was strategic investment, or if the foreign bank would have a say in decision-making too. The answer the deputy governor gave was 'strategic investment'. And the deal was allowed to go through, as foreign investors, at that time, were permitted to make strategic investments in banks.

Later, the chairman of the private bank, who was a former Indian Administrative Service (IAS) officer, came running to Reddy and pleaded for the bank to be saved from the predator. The governor was furious. He knew the intention of the foreign bank, and, therefore, had asked if it wanted to be just a strategic investor or have a say in the management. And the chairman himself had said that it was a strategic investor. So angry was the governor that he called this 'corporate fraud'. The chairperson of the foreign bank knew that until Reddy was in the governor's chair, he would not allow this investor to get the bank. The investor could do nothing in Mumbai, so they would run to Delhi and abuse the governor in the corridors of power. So much so that once the press advisor of the prime minister told me that, as a communication advisor to the governor, I should advise him to speak more and reveal his mind. The governor, of course, knew this. But he believed that actions spoke louder than words. If the policies implemented by him were for the welfare of the nation, then he need not defend himself. He was intellectually honest and would not compromise the policies that he thought were right for the country, no matter what the financial world wanted to believe was right.

I once again urged the governor to brief the media informally on this issue—how a foreign bank was surreptitiously trying to take over an Indian bank. He reluctantly agreed to brief the media, and we arranged an informal meeting. Reddy was quite unrestrained and we allowed portions of the briefing to be reported, too, albeit anonymously. Unfortunately, no journalist reported the episode. I still have not understood why. To me it sounded like a scoop. Of course, as expected, he did not allow the foreign bank to take over the Indian bank. But that a well-reputed foreign bank tried to surreptitiously acquire a private bank and that the Indian bank's chairperson was hand in glove in the coup remained hidden from the world.

Caution Gave Him Abuses but Saved India

Reddy was openly conservative and believed in going ahead slowly but surely on the path to reform, rather than moving rapidly and then backtracking. He would tell us, 'Financial markets can recover fast, but not the economy.' And so he would rather go slow on a path that was not too familiar. The markets, as always, did not want to see this point. They wanted India to quickly open up for foreign investments, especially to foreign institutional investors, like pension funds and overseas corporate bodies, and rush to capital account convertibility. The market also thought it was ready for financial innovations like securitization, which the developed world was already trading in. They obviously did not like Reddy's cautious and slow approach. The so-called bright and progressive minds in the world of finance would go to Delhi and complain bitterly against the RBI and, particularly, the governor. Worse still, he very rarely explained his stance to the market through speeches, which was an accepted way of communication for the RBI.

In fact, Reddy saw the global financial crisis of 2008 coming even before the world could see it. I clearly remember this. He had just returned from one of the bi-monthly BIS meetings. I happened to meet him just then. He narrated some part of the discussion to me which sounded ominous. The expressions on his face made me realize the seriousness of what he was saying. I suggested to him that we brief the press about it right away so that they were prepared for the worst to come and, in their own way, could prepare the financial system and the country for it. For some reason, he agreed. Otherwise, the understanding between us was that we were not to use the press to build public opinion. I guess that understanding was related to policies; and *this* was not just policy. What he had gathered by talking to the central bankers in Basel, Switzerland, was the simmer of a full-blown financial crisis.

We called representatives of mainly the financial press. I remember. It was so sudden, we could not even get a proper meeting room for the press briefing. So, it was held in the room where the governor's executive assistant would sit. There were less chairs than media persons; so, they stood. But no one complained. They were more interested in what the governor had to say. He spoke for almost an hour and a half to them. It was a monologue and the media was listening. When he finished, there was pin-drop silence. Briefly, he had just told them about how the banks in the US had messed up their home-loan portfolios by bundling them into big tickets and selling them to other institutional investors, such as the pension funds and insurance companies. He foresaw the failure of the big institutions, though the first failure (of Lehman Brothers) came only after he left the RBI. He went to attend the next BIS meeting two months later and described how the Bank of England governor had backed out from the meeting at the last moment. 'Something is wrong… I can tell you… Otherwise, having confirmed his participation in the meeting, the Bank of England governor wouldn't have backed out like this,' he told us. A few days later, news of the Northern Rock failure hit the world. Reddy's conjecture had proved right.

While the world stared at the global financial crisis in the aftermath of the collapse of Lehman Brothers (2008), the Indian financial system stood rock solid. On seeing the first sign of a bubble forming in the Indian real-estate market, Reddy had already made credit dearer for this sector. This was again a masterstroke from the master administrator. Generally, the RBI used measures like CRR and SLR to make money dearer when the economy heated up. These measures would, however, hit all the sectors of the economy and the economy as a whole would slow down. If we were to take such general measures, economic growth would have suffered, and the RBI would have been criticized bitterly for hurting growth. The problem also was restricted only to real estate. So, Reddy thought of measures that would make credit more expensive only for real estate loans. He took administrative measures as opposed to monetary measures to slow down the flow of credit to real estate. He increased the margin and risk weights for loans against real estate. This would mean banks would have to keep aside more capital when they extended loans to real estate. This was perhaps the first time administrative measures were used as a monetary tool. He had also not allowed securitization in Indian markets. India had nothing to worry about.

Much later, all those who had called Reddy names thanked him for saving India's financial system. Going slowly and carefully towards capital account convertibility and allowing financial innovation, such as securitization, barring foreign investments in critical sectors like banking, and banning overseas corporate bodies, were all applauded by the likes of IMF and other respected names in the financial world. Nobel Laureate Joseph Stiglitz, in a public speech, acknowledged Reddy's wisdom by saying, 'If only America had a central bank chief like Y.V. Reddy, the US economy would not have been such a mess.'[3] This was not happening for the first time. In 1997, when the Asian crisis hit, India had not hesitated in raising the wall around itself to stall outward capital flow. While the world criticized the RBI for being slow in reforming the economy, Jalan and Reddy stood firm.

'There is no harm in stepping back for a while if there are problems. One can always come back and start again from where one had left,' he had said then as the deputy governor.

Delhi's *Dadagiri*

And yet, in the fifth year of his term, Reddy decided that enough was enough. He went to the finance minister and told him to look for his successor, as he was not interested in a second term.

The problem, in my view, was that neither the government nor the RBI did much to build public opinion in favour of policies. We did no PR on the policy side either. Often, explaining policies would help get the support of the stakeholders, but not doing it resulted in a near breakdown in the government–RBI relationship. So much so that some believed that the bureaucrats in the government had started

---

[3]Bajaj, Vikas, 'In India, Central Banker Played It Safe', *The New York Times*, 25 June 2009, https://tinyurl.com/4s75p5bx. Accessed on 30 October 2023.

conspiring against the RBI. One senior bureaucrat who, first secretly and then openly, aspired to be the governor of the RBI even went to the extent of saying that he would reduce the RBI to a government department before he retired. The bureaucrat fell out of favour with the next finance minister and retired unsung. The bureaucrats even took help from some learned people to give theoretical ground to their vicious arguments against the RBI stance. Of course, all this was journalistic chatter in the corridors of the powers that be. But I always believed that there was no smoke without fire.

During Reddy's tenure as the governor, there were so many contentious issues—whether the RBI should increase or decrease interest rates, allowing foreign investments through participatory notes, taking away the management of government debt from the RBI and setting up an independent office within the government to take over this function, auditing the policy operations of the RBI by the Comptroller and Auditor General (CAG), using foreign exchange reserves for infrastructure development, not allowing revision of pension to RBI staff. The list seemed endless. All in all, Delhi's *dadagiri* (bullying) was increasing day by day. But Reddy would not budge on policies.

Visitors to RBI

Reddy was very fond of travelling. As deputy governor and as governor, he would undertake travel at the drop of a hat. Or so we all felt. The market talk, however, was that when Jalan was the governor, he and Reddy, who was the deputy governor, did not see eye to eye on several issues. And so, Reddy preferred to remain out to avoid conflicts. This smoke had some fire as the former was a liberal and the latter a conservative when it came to reforms. Whatever be the reason, Reddy's excursions brought a lot of visibility for the RBI. He got invited to many other central banks, and when he visited them, he must have extended invitations to them in typical Indian tradition. And as India came slowly into prominence—first for its resistance to the world's opinion in implementing full capital account convertibility and later for its slow but steady pace of reforms due to which it had emerged unscathed from the global financial crisis—the flow of visitors to India and to the RBI increased. We saw and interacted with the likes of heads of many central banks and well-known economists. And we could see the respect they had for India and for Reddy. They all came to learn from the Indian experience. The RBI was being watched closely for the policy experiments it was doing.

Communication Given Its Due

Amidst all these, Reddy gave communication its rightful place. He did not believe in building opinion but he did believe in communication. When he was the deputy governor, he got me to write the basic document on communication policy for the RBI. It was more of a dissemination policy than a communication policy. When I mentioned this to Reddy, he simply said, 'But something, maa…Then you build upon it and write the communication policy…'

The RBI published a lot of data and research. These were published unevenly, and much of it went unnoticed. As deputy governor, Reddy had got the research department to build a kind of calendar for publications and data we released. He even brought it into public domain by including it in a speech on communication made under the auspices of a news wire agency. Between the governor and I, we called it dissemination policy—a precursor to the RBI's communication policy. Reddy publicly acknowledged my contribution to the communication function by calling me the 'point person' for communication in the RBI in that speech.

There was a little side story behind the speech. One day, the chief of the foreign news wire agency Reuters asked me for an appointment with Reddy, the deputy governor. He refused to tell me what it was about; I knew that was the first question Reddy would ask me whenever I went to him with some media request. But the gentleman refused to tell me the purpose. This was common—journalists often treat PR professionals with disdain. So, I did not take such denials to heart and went to Reddy with the blank request.

Reddy got suspicious. I told him that the chief had refused to divulge what it was about. We both suspected something fishy in his reluctance to share the agenda of the meeting. So, Reddy told me to fob him off. I called him back and told him that the governor would't be able to see him as he was quite busy and was travelling abroad that night. The chief was gritty. He said he would wait as long as the governor wanted him to, but meet Reddy he must. This to and fro went on till 8 p.m. with call-check every half hour or so. Finally, Reddy was left with no choice. He asked me to get him in within the next 15 minutes. We both thought that the chief would not be able to make it in such a short time and so we would get our way.

To our surprise he showed up in the next 10 minutes! And the purpose, too, was quite benign. He wanted to invite him for a function celebrating the agency's 150th anniversary celebration. We were relieved; Reddy, too, didn't require much persuasion to agree. This was where he gave the speech. I think that was the first speech ever on the subject of communication for the RBI. All in all, the entire episode had the communication function at its centre.

Giving Access

As the governor, Reddy opened all doors for me, the spokesperson of the RBI. I was free to attend any open meeting held in the RBI. This formalized after some time; I would get formal invitations to attend meetings to which outsiders were invited. This helped me in my job tremendously. I could understand the rationale behind policies that were being formulated. A side benefit was that I could respond to media queries about such meetings without cross-checking with anyone.

The RBI was still shrouded in mystery, and outsiders, especially media, were always curious to know what was going on. So when meetings were held with bankers or other stakeholders, media invariably asked them about what transpired at the meetings. Outsiders almost always obliged them and briefed them. Of course, being in a conservative institution like the RBI, I consciously did not adopt a proactive approach in my role as communication officer. I never called the media to brief them about such meetings. But if someone called me and asked, I ensured that he/she was led on the correct path about the discussions that took place. I believed this raised my stature in the eyes of the media. Senior journalists would always ask their junior colleagues if they had spoken to me when it came to banking or central banking. I learnt a lot about the intricacies of banking, finance and administration during Reddy's time.

Media Management

When Reddy had taken charge as the governor, he had clearly told me, 'As governor, I would encourage the deputy governors to speak to the media.' The deputies, however, preferred to stay away from the media, as perhaps they assumed that the governor might not like it if they were interacting with them. The RBI, that way, is a curious institution. Everyone tries to second-guess and assume what the person above wants, and behaves accordingly. The word about whom the governor likes and whom he does not goes around very quickly, and that can change the attitude of others towards you equally quickly. Reddy's affection and kindness towards me helped me a great deal in my functioning. I could do a lot in the communication space with his support.

That Governor Reddy would not be accessible to the media was a big change in RBI's communication policy, since, as the deputy governor, Reddy used to be very accessible. This meant quite a lot of explaining to the media. He loved to travel and talk. He kept receiving invitations—as deputy governor and as governor—to speak. There were several invitations from other central banks too. So, he would be out of office frequently. He would travel a lot as the deputy governor, much to the chagrin of his governor, Jalan. So much so that towards the end of Reddy's tenure as the deputy governor, media started speculating that all was not well between Reddy and Jalan.

It was altogether a different matter that many media persons did not understand much of what he spoke. Not because the media wasn't smart. But Reddy often spoke in half sentences and in riddles. 'Constructive ambiguity', he would call it, turning around the phrase often used at that time in the context of monetary policy. It, in fact, became an expression to describe the RBI's monetary policy stance during his tenure. His quick wit and articulation were unparalleled. With both, he would spin a yarn out of the most difficult question and wriggle out without making the journalist realize a thing. He was a wordsmith.

We took many initiatives in media management around this time—for example, training media personnel in the matters of the RBI. It was his idea to do it, and to do it in one of our training colleges. Reddy had explained to me the advantage of conducting the training in a training establishment. 'Give them that feel, maa,' he would say. In a training environment, they would take the training seriously and the temptation for reporting something would be less. My take was that the journalists would be completely free from their work responsibilities and would be able to focus on learning. Receiving their nominations from their organizations would thus indicate how serious the news organization was about training its staff in central banking. The advantage to the RBI was greater accuracy in reporting on central banking issues.

There were two training colleges of the RBI—one in Pune and the other in Chennai. Pune was a better choice than Chennai because it was closer to Mumbai. Media persons would find it easier to travel to Pune than to Chennai. Reddy had also told me to get the college to waive the lodging charges and tuition fees and to get the media houses to pay only for the media persons' travel. This was his way of ensuring that the media houses took this as a serious learning affair and not just some junket.

However, I could not put the training idea into action at the time, as neither of the training colleges would give me a slot. For them, communication was perhaps a peripheral function and media a necessary evil that could not be wished away. Every time the governor asked me what happened, I would cut a sorry figure. He, perhaps, understood my difficulty without being told. One fine day, the regime at the college in Pune changed. There was a new principal, and in a casual conversation Reddy told me to ask the college again for a slot, adding that the incumbent would be more pliable. And I instantly knew that it would work. The new principal was an HR man himself and understood the media well. When he was the executive assistant to Jalan, we had taken many initiatives in communication. More importantly, he was a very good leader. I got the slot and the first batch of around 25 journalists, mainly from Mumbai, representing all financial newspapers, television channels and wire agencies, reported to the Pune college. The two-faculty team at the college was also young and was thrilled to take up this new challenge.

As instructed by Reddy, we got the college to waive the fees for lodging, study material and classes. I had curated the training keeping both sides in mind. The journalists would be taught a bit of theory by the college faculty—who also were RBI officers incidentally—as well as given a glimpse of the current thinking in each and every function of the Bank by the incumbent head of the function. This, for the media, had some news value. The functional heads clarified many current issues that journalists otherwise did not bother or did not have time to understand or verify in their daily grind. The training also gave something substantive to the trainee journalists to carry back to their offices. The mutual understanding was that whenever the journalists wrote about the discussed issues or functions in the future, they could use the material and the insights gathered at these sessions but without quoting the officer or the sessions. The journalists were also allowed to follow the leads that they might have picked up in the sessions and file a story later after some research. They were asked not to report about the educative sessions per se. That is, they could not say that the RBI had organized a training session for the media, and so on.

The journalists loved these training sessions as they improved their understanding of the RBI and gave them 'access' to the Bank's functionaries. Or so they thought. I actually briefed the officers about the 'access' obsession of the journalists and told them not to carry their visiting cards to these sessions. Most officers abided by my advice and pointed towards me when the journalists asked for their contacts. They could also connect in the future with the faculty in the college for their queries, since for theoretical background, we depended on the college staff. For the college, though, it became heavy-duty stuff as they had to manage not only the journalists but also heads of departments—two or three at a time—as they arrived from Mumbai for their sessions. Yet, there was excitement on both sides, which was a great start.

The first course rocked. The journalists went back satisfied, to say the least. No one even thought of or mentioned the possibility of any ulterior motive behind this training. It was all about learning. In fact, it was much later that I learnt that, at times, when media houses would refuse to pay for the journalists' travel and tell them to ask the RBI to pay for it, some of them would take leave from work and pay for the journey themselves to come for the training but would not ask the RBI to bear the cost. For the heads of departments, too, interacting with journalists was a novel experience. They had always been reticent and somewhat afraid too, and therefore, indifferent to the media. Some of them later appreciated my presence in those sessions, as they knew that there was someone to 'save' them if journalists played mischief by reporting the discussions. I would sit through all the sessions just to ensure that neither the RBI officials dropped their guard nor did any of the journalists get up to any mischief. I was quite confident about the journalists. Many of them had told me that they would never breach the RBI's confidence, or mine. They never did—in training or otherwise.

What a learning it was! At times, the heads of departments excelled themselves while talking about why they did what they did. They were simply mesmerizing. A session I clearly remember was taken by Prashant Saran, the then head of banking regulation. My request to him was to explain to the journalists the philosophy behind bank regulation. He was most reluctant to meet and address the journalists. When I pursued him, he asked me what should he speak on. So I gave him a very rough outline—the way I had understood the philosophy behind bank regulation. He relented. After the introduction, he started talking. And what a talk it was! Sheer poetry on bank regulation! It was magical. I wish I had recorded that speech. Unfortunately, today, neither Saran nor I remember what he spoke. I realized that such jewels should be preserved for posterity.

The formal five-day training sessions for the media in our Pune college became quite popular. There was always demand for these programmes. But we could organize only two such training courses in a year. We observed that it was always media from Mumbai that attended these sessions; media from other centres, though keen, could not make it for some reason or the other. So, later, we started going to other centres with the same programme. Although, these being only half as successful as those conducted at the home base, media persons often got called back from the sessions by their employers for some spot reporting. The temptation to report the sessions was also high. 'Reserve Bank *ki meeting thi. Kuchh to report karna padega* (It was a Reserve Bank meeting. Something must be reported)' was the usual demand from the editors. So I would tell them to report on currency matters, which would also interest their local readers. Later, we received a request from the Nepal Rashtra Bank—Nepal's central bank—to conduct these sessions for the Nepalese media. We did two or three such training programmes for them over time.

Communication Policy

As Reddy's tenure as governor came to a close, he also got me to write the communication policy for the Bank. This time, it was the actual communication policy and not the dissemination policy that we had written earlier. There were some norms that I would follow to communicate with the media. But these were informal and had no approval of any kind. It was just that these norms had worked well for me and for the RBI. There was not much of a communication policy in them. But he insisted I write it down. So, between the monetary policy department and me, we drafted a communication policy. The department provided the theory of central bank communication and I wrote what we were actually practising. In the RBI, for some reason, people are averse to giving or taking credit. So even if the current practices were what I had devised, I never called it my work and just termed it as a compilation of existing practices. The policy got approved by the Board and was published on the RBI website as the communication policy.

The policy contained simple tenets like explaining the issue and stance but never to aim to be quoted. A quote meant using my name, and once you allow that, they would want a photo. Both meant personal publicity, and the RBI by culture is publicity-shy. I also shunned all media requests for getting my views on RBI policies. I would argue that, in RBI, we didn't distinguish between the self and the institution. We would express our views in meetings and on policy notes. But once a decision was taken, we all fell in line and carried the same view as that of the institution. The other principle was that the press releases would be issued only by the central office in Mumbai, where the Bank's top management sat and which made the policies. This established a single line of communication for the RBI.

Later, we included heads of the regional offices to clarify local issues. Generally, the local media would call the regional office and seek clarifications on local issues, which were usually related to currency and coins. The regional office would direct them to me. I would get back to the regional office, obtain the clarification and articulate it to the local media. This was quite circuitous. So, it was decided that regional offices would rather clarify these issues to local media. However, soon I realized that speaking to the media was not everyone's cup of tea. Some were not confident, some not articulate and some were oversmart and spoke too much, creating unnecessary noise. I lobbied to include at least one session of media training for the newly promoted regional heads, and got it done.

The communication policy got updated after almost 10 years—in 2021. Sadly, the policy as it is published on the RBI's website does not contain a few tenets we prescribed for members of the Central Board and also for the members of the Monetary Policy Committee (MPC). The tenets were written and approved but were kept in the respective departments—those for Board members lie in the files of the Secretary's Department and those for MPC members remain in the Monetary Policy Department—and never made their way to the Department of Communication and to the communication policy on the website. I have heard that they are shared only with the members of the Central Board and the MPC. This is a typical central banker mindset. They think departmentally and not functionally. How else could one explain that the communication policy for the Central Board member or for an MPC member resided in the respective departments and not in the communication department? Ideally, it should have been on both the departments' records.

Communicating in Local Languages

A far-reaching change Reddy tried to make in the way the RBI communicated was to introduce regional language communication. We started interacting with regional media during press conferences held to announce the monetary policy. The video conference facility, which was just being introduced in India, came handy for interactions with the regional media. After the announcement of every monetary policy, the regional offices would invite the regional media representatives to their offices to interact with the RBI governor. The governor would try to speak to them in their language. He could speak many languages. He was obviously fluent in Telugu, that being his mother tongue. He could also speak Tamil, a smattering of Malayalam and some Hindi. His use of '*dal-chawal to khana hai na* (one has to eat rice and lentils)' to explain the concept of inflation became a headline, just like Raghuram Rajan's '*dosa* economics' later became the talk of the town.

At the back end though, communicating with the regional media was quite a task. The first issue was technology. Being new and not too widely used, it was the first hurdle to cross. Second, communication with so many centres was a marathon task. Communication with the regional media first started with four metro cities. Other centres got added gradually. Even if we kept 10–15 minutes for each centre, the four metros—Mumbai, Delhi, Kolkata and Chennai—themselves took about an hour. The time got added to the main press conference that was held for about an hour and a half in Mumbai with the Mumbai media. While Reddy thoroughly enjoyed talking to the regional media, for others—the Mumbai press and the RBI officials attending the conference in Mumbai and other regional centres—it became too strenuous and, perhaps, boring and tiring to sit through. For regional centres, the practice was an additional burden, as the regional media hardly followed the RBI's monetary policy. Their concern was mostly limited to currency notes and co-operative banks operating in their state. So, getting them to attend the press conference was a huge task for the regional heads. Most of the time there would be two to three press persons in regional offices. So that the room did not look empty, regional offices would get some of their own officers to sit through the press conference. On top of that, the officers in the regional offices also had to prepare and pass on to the media an intelligent-sounding question or two—intelligent enough for a governor to answer.

From video conference technology we graduated to conference call facility for the regional media. I wrote to all the regional offices explaining the conferencing technology, telling them that, with this technology, the media would be able to call into the press conference from their own offices or homes, and that the offices would not need to invite media persons over. Several of the regional heads called me up and thanked me for saving them from the drudgery of calling and briefing the media in their offices. One regional head shared with me that he had to cajole the local media to come, give them intelligent questions to ask and, at the end, summarize the press conference and the governor's response to their questions in Tamil, as economics and monetary policy were not the local press persons' cup of tea. I could understand this. Since the RBI was headquartered in Mumbai, it was the responsibility of the Mumbai bureau of all national media houses to report on the RBI. The regional bureaus were not expected to cover the central bank. And so, they never looked at the RBI and were hardly aware of the developments, just as Reddy was unaware of the struggle officers at the regional centres had to put up with.

During that time, we also started doing elaborate interviews with financial media after the monetary policy was announced. It would mainly be the business television channels and newspapers. Reddy would go through them all very patiently, emerging victorious. I thought, somewhere, this helped communication because the messages got repeated multiple times. At times, though, I did wish we were selective in giving interviews; but I would not have been able to do this myself without the governor's explicit backing.

Fatigue at the End

During Reddy's tenure as the governor, he was bitterly criticized by the bankers. The media would simply report what the bankers told them to. The result was that Reddy had to constantly explain his stance to the government on the one hand and to the media on the other. Such was the badgering that, towards the fifth year of his tenure, he looked visibly tired and drawn down. The institutional differences between the government and the RBI spilled out in the public domain, and media hyped these to the hilt. Naturally, Reddy decided to complete his five-year term and did not want any extension.

The institutional differences between the government and the RBI are intrinsic to the nature and purpose of the two institutions. One is political, elected and has a five-year perspective at the most. The other is apolitical, appointed and has a long-term perspective. And India is not the only country to have its government dominate over the central bank. The basic difference between the two, as Reddy would often explain, is that one is elected and the other is appointed. The appointed will, thus, always be answerable to the elected. The media, interested in a daily byline, tends to play one against the other. In short, each institution plays the role assigned to it. Who wins in this game? Rather, who loses in this game? India, for sure, has lost the best minds to this clash—be it Venkitaramanan, Reddy or Raghuram Rajan. And the struggle continues.

5

Duvvuri Subbarao

From Delhi to Mumbai

Dr Duvvuri Subbarao (2008–2013) entered the RBI during a tumultuous time. The relations between the government and the RBI had completely soured. He was finance secretary at the time when Reddy was governor. So, when the government announced his name as governor, the media was quick to proclaim him as the finance ministry man and waited to see the undermining of the RBI's autonomy.

There was also chatter in the informal circles that there was a coterie in the finance ministry working against the RBI. Two economists, who were part of a reputed research hub, and one bureaucrat worked tirelessly to cut the wings of the RBI, so to speak. They tried everything to curb the independence of the Bank. The economist duo gave a theoretical cover to their arguments and the bureaucrat ensured those arguments reached the finance minister's ears. It was also alleged that the finance ministry paid a huge sum to the research hub to finance the research duo's work against the RBI. With that money, they conducted seminars and spoke openly and nastily against the Bank's independence. But all this was never confirmed.

Initially, when Subbarao took over as the governor, he had to divide his time between two major events—one, monitoring the developments with regard to the global financial crisis, and two, the platinum jubilee celebrations of the central bank. Governor Subbarao had walked straight into the global financial crisis. Though the crisis had started brewing in Reddy's time, the first manifestation of it—the collapse of Lehman Brothers—came one week into him taking over as the governor. Since the crisis was out in the open, the first task was to check our own backyard to see if there was something that needed attention. Thanks to Reddy's conservative policies, the Indian financial system was virtually unaffected. But no one would want to believe that. So, 'second-rung effect', 'can India be affected in the second round?' and 'what should be done to protect India from that?' were matters of daily discussion in the RBI and outside. RBI would meet bankers and other stakeholders of finance industry almost every alternate day and ask what was needed to protect the Indian financial system and prevent it from being affected. Like the finance ministry, Subbarao also, perhaps, initially thought that the Bank was too rigid and hard to crack. The belief manifested in a certain way. Many were of the opinion that he would listen to outsiders but not to the RBI staff, or, even if he did, he would listen to them only dismissively.

I very clearly remember one such meeting with the bankers. Subbarao and all the deputy governors, the executive director and the department head in charge of regulation were present. I was there too. The agenda was the same. Was India's banking industry being affected by the crisis even a small bit? What needed to be done? Were there any precautions that needed to be taken? Come any crisis and the first thing the bankers would ask, and so did the RBI, was whether enough money—liquidity—was available in the financial system. The RBI had already put in place some lines of credit to provide liquidity to certain sectors that had links with the outside world. These were not being utilized yet. But when the governor asked the bankers if the RBI could do anything more, the bankers were prompt in forwarding a list of more things—mainly, more money, lower interest rates and more concessions.

At this juncture, one of the deputy governors pointed out to the bankers that the earlier facilities were not even being utilized, implying that the bankers should not be asking for more. The senior-most banker at the table promptly retorted that 'acquiring a fire extinguisher does not mean there is a fire!' I had never seen or heard bankers talking to RBI officials so brusquely. The governor, too, in a somewhat stern voice admonished the concerned deputy governor, saying that the RBI was in the room in a 'listening mode'.

There was a reason for turning on the 'listening mode' that Subbarao kept telling us about. Just before he came to Mumbai to take over as the RBI governor, he had met with Manmohan Singh, the prime minister of India at that time. Singh had advised him to keep his ears to the ground, saying that, in the RBI, one could lose touch with the ground. Subbarao followed this advice sincerely and did everything possible to get the RBI to feel the ground. He would, in fact, tell the RBI officials to be in a 'listening mode' before every meeting with outsiders.

This started changing slowly as Subbarao met more officials in the RBI and heard them. Towards the end of his tenure, he was convinced that the RBI worked selflessly in the interest of the system and started defending it in all forums. Many thought that by the time he left the RBI, his views on most matters were diametrically opposite to what the finance ministry thought on these issues. That's how, when a journalist asked him in his exit interview about when he changed his views, he had promptly answered, 'In the flight from Delhi to Mumbai.'

Demystifying the RBI

Subbarao was keen on demystifying the RBI. One such occasion was provided by its platinum jubilee. The RBI completed the seventy-fifth year of its existence in the year 2010. This was about a year and a half into Subbarao's tenure as governor. The global financial crisis was not yet behind us, but the fire was not blazing any more. It was now a question of 'taper tantrum', or handling the fallout of withdrawing the liquidity that the central banks world over had let loose in the system. This gave some breathing space to the top management. There were initially no plans to celebrate the platinum jubilee. The foundation day of the RBI, 1 April 2010, passed by very quietly.

In some corners though, there was some clamouring about the big event. Slowly, this clamour started building up. The idea was quite hazy when we started. We also started quite late in the year. The first function we celebrated was in September 2010 in the form of a discussion among all the living governors. The event was held in Hyderabad because most of the past governors happened to be living there—M. Narasimham, C. Rangarajan and Y.V. Reddy. Bimal Jalan flew in from Delhi. Unfortunately, Venkitaramanan could not participate for health reasons. The celebration, with financial literacy as its central theme, had communication writ large on it; but, initially, the Department of Communication was nowhere in the scene.

The RBI's regional office in Hyderabad was organizing the event. Media coverage, too, was initially being handled by the regional office, but I had to force myself into the event for media coverage. When I reached the venue of the event, there was chaos all around, as far as the media was concerned. The arrangements for the media were not at all favourable for a good coverage. To begin with, all media were invited, but they were not assigned any specific space. Therefore, they were all over the place. Still photographers were complaining about video cameras, while the reporters and the audience were complaining about cameramen causing disturbance with their flash lights. The situation was just about explosive. Somehow, we managed to salvage the situation, but the coverage of such a unique event was not at all satisfactory—it was patchy and did not receive the kind of traction that a platinum jubilee celebration of the country's central bank being graced by five governors should have received.

There were at least three valuable lessons for me to learn on communication from this event. First, assign a specific space to the media persons in general and especially to media persons with cameras. Video cameras can manage distances, so they can be placed somewhere in the middle or end of the room; still photographers can be in the front for a few minutes and then guided to another designated place. Second, partnership with one media house can work better in the coverage of an event of this scale and this kind. For a public body like the RBI, this can be tricky, as excluding any media is not a possibility. Yet, it was important to record and telecast the entire discussion simply because it had five governors on the dais. And third, it is imperative that such high-level discussions are preserved for posterity.

As an organization also, we learnt from this event. The world outside hardly knew about the RBI and the role it played in the common man's daily life. Slowly, this started building up as the theme of the celebration. Each department was asked to suggest events and prepare an action plan. These were discussed and finalized in what we called the top management committee. That's when financial literacy emerged as the full-fledged theme for the celebration. The financial literacy drive was given two dimensions—one relating to banking and the other relating to the Bank, or the RBI. Subbarao was very keen that we 'demystify' central banking. At some point, he narrated the Manmohan Singh story to us and told us how this experience had prompted him to think of 'demystifying' the RBI as one of the two themes for the platinum jubilee celebrations.

Communication Was the Centrepiece

Communication was implied in the theme, and the Department of Communication contributed the most to the ongoing celebrations. It not only planned the maximum number of events in coordination with the media but also helped arrange publicity for events organized by regional offices and departments. To the credit of the media, each business channel wanted to plan an event to commemorate the seventy-fifth year of the central bank. And all of them wanted to have a panel of past RBI governors on their channel. Subbarao was very supportive of this. He agreed to write a letter to all the living ex-governors—some seven of them—and invite them to participate in the events.

Initially, we toyed with the idea of doing just one event with one business channel. Being the central bank, however, we had to be equitable and transparent so that no one could point a finger and accuse us of partiality. We had to steer clear of the vigilance angle too. So, we floated a tender and invited all the channels to bid for the event. The bids were to be evaluated on the basis of the concept. We offered not money, but what we had—a panel of past governors and the incumbent one, or a panel of the governor and all deputy governors. The channels were supposed to bring what was their strength—the concept of an event and its production.

The idea worked. Each business channel came up with a brilliant concept, and instead of one event with one media house, we decided to do an event with each one of them. Alongside the event, each channel also produced a short film paying tribute to the central bank. One channel traced the evolution of the central bank through different governors, another did a film on the RBI through some major financial crises. No channel asked for any money from the RBI, except one. We could have prevailed over that channel, too, but the deputy governor in charge of that event was kind and sanctioned the additional budget. The panel discussions were telecast on their channel along with the short film they had made on the central bank.

Apart from this, we did town halls in which the governor and the deputy governors appeared as a panel before the students or general public and answered their questions. For these events, too, we put the same idea to work. We offered the channels the panel of topmost officials, and they were to do a ground-level event, bringing common people or students to ask questions. The questions ranged from monetary policy to exchange rate and supervisory issues. Sometimes, a seemingly innocent question would really be tricky to answer in an open format. For instance, in the Chennai event, a taxi driver was in the audience. His question was: why couldn't the RBI take care of black money? Now, the RBI has no role to play in the creation or curbing of black money, as it is a fallout of tax regime and is thus in the realm of the government. This was tricky, as in an open format we could not have said it was the government's business, and not the RBI's, to curb black money. I don't remember the exact words in which the question was answered. But a reply to the question was given.

Another initiative under financial literacy was conducting a quiz for school children in grades 8, 9 and 10. It was logistically a very big event. With the support of the regional offices of the RBI, the quiz was conducted at the state level. Winner teams were sent for regional-level participation and from there to the national level. We designed a television programme of five episodes to cover semi-finals and finals, with one episode called the 'curtain raiser'. We conducted the quiz for three years. The first year's programme was covered by a private channel. And after that, for the next two years, the programmes were taken over by Doordarshan, the state-owned public service broadcaster.

Many of these events were done on heritage sites and in institutions at different centres. These sites were owned by the state governments, such as the Government Museum, Chennai, popularly known as the Egmore Museum; the Rock Garden in Chandigarh; the Asiatic Society Library in Mumbai; and the National Library in Kolkata. As such, the venue did not cost us any money. Chunks of these events were telecast live and later edited and telecast as a half-hour or 40-minute capsule by the channels over weekends. To gain the maximum mileage out of these events, we also put up a financial literacy exhibition around the physical events using the open spaces of these iconic premises.

We published a coffee-table book on the RBI, and a brochure and a small book describing its role and functions. So much interesting material was collected for the coffee-table book that we decided to use some of it to set up an exhibition. This exhibition, on the role and functions of the RBI, turned out to be a crowd-puller, and we converted it into a travelling exhibition that travelled to many more cities than originally planned. An objective of centrally creating the exhibition was to bring in uniformity in messages and creativity. However, each office, including the training colleges, was also putting up an exhibition of its own in the name of financial literacy. Events for the employees—past and present—were conducted at the department and the regional office levels.

The celebrations had both internal and external events. Internally, each department was asked to organize at least one event to which all the living employees who had retired from that department were to be invited. Each department recorded its evolution with photographs and file notings either in book form or in video form—done in-house of course—which made all of it a great collection for the Bank's archives. There was also socializing for the departmental people. The retired staff and officials were quite happy to be included in the celebration.

The entire episode highlighted one more issue to me. As every office and every department was taking an initiative to create something, they were all using the creativity of some of their own staff. While it encouraged talent and saved money for the RBI, it also had diverse messages and a wide variety of designs, colours and style—some were good, and some were not. As a communication person, I resented the inconsistency the variety brought with it, but the excitement and involvement of the staff made it more than acceptable. It was also physically not possible to control everything at the Department of Communication. And some creations were indeed top-class, like the film on financial literacy that one of the staff members from a regional office had conceptualized and executed. It simply depicted two women—one who took a bank loan and slowly improved her living condition and the other who didn't and remained in her hand-to-mouth condition. Sadly, all these later got buried—hopefully in the archives—with no updation, except for the book on the role and functions of the RBI, which was reluctantly updated almost a decade later by the staff training college in Chennai.

The celebration culminated in an international conference on financial literacy, in coordination with the Paris-based Organisation for Economic Co-operation and Development (OECD). This again had the Department of Communication spearheading the event. OECD had been doing some good work in the financial literacy area. We managed to get the finance minister to inaugurate the conference and some eminent speakers from India and abroad to grace the occasion, along with a good participation from central banks of several other countries.

Village Immersion

Subbarao always believed in first-hand experiences. So, he insisted on creating some lasting programme for financial inclusion. Each regional office was asked to adopt a few villages and, with the support of the lead bank and district authorities, ensure a bank account for all the households in those villages. As per the governor's order, one top executive—either the governor himself or one of the deputy governors or the executive directors—was required to be involved in the efforts of the regional office. There was virtually a competition among the regional offices to invite the governor or the deputy governors to their offices. He instructed the offices and the officers not to be pompous at these events. He even asked the men to go for such events in a plain shirt and pants rather than a suit and a tie.

Subbarao himself chose Odisha (then Orissa) for mentoring. Having worked at the grassroots level as a district collector, he knew how to work at that level. The RBI officials, along with district-level government officials and bankers, would visit the village, and the banks would open accounts in bulk for the people in that village. This was the RBI's own version of Jan Dhan Yojana but without the name and the fanfare that the government later brought. So involved was Subbarao in this activity that, while visiting a girls' school in Odisha, he himself started teaching the basics of central banking to the students.

The only negative thing about these events was that the villagers did not know what the RBI was. And so, whenever a large group of RBI officials would visit the village, they were mistaken for government officials and presented with complaints that were administrative in nature. This would take the focus away from financial literacy and inclusion, which were the main objectives of this initiative. However, this did not negate the gains of the RBI's initiative. Later, when the government announced its Jan Dhan Yojana, the media and the people at large were already aware of what the scheme was all about, and it naturally met with huge success.

For the base-level officers in the RBI, too, we started a village immersion programme during Subbarao's tenure. A select group of young, fresh recruits were to do a two-month village immersion programme and write a report based on their experience in the village. They were required to live in that village, instead of commuting daily from the town, for the entirety of those two months. These reports would be evaluated by a panel of senior officers and the best three would get a cash prize. The first prize was one lakh rupees, which was a great reward for beginners. As one of the members of the jury, I got to read these essays, and I found some of them to be simply brilliant. The suggestions they had made were very practical and worthy of implementation. But I don't think they were even considered at the department level in the RBI. Like other such initiatives, this initiative too slowly petered out.

Incognito Visits to Bank Branches

One more push to 'touching base with reality' came in the form of Subbarao asking all the senior officials participating in the senior management meeting to visit bank branches incognito and ask for some service or the other to gauge if the service was being delivered. 'You are all shortly going to be senior citizens and will be visiting bank branches for your own work,' he would say, coaxing us into experiencing what we were going to get after a few years, while in service. The purpose of these visits was to improve customer service in banks. The changes brought about by the RBI in rules and regulations towards better customer service were not reaching the ground and benefitting the common man. Many of us did what Subbarao had asked, and most of us came back agitated at not getting the expected service. There was a large gap between the rules and their delivery, which sadly exists even today. That last mile, till date, remains unserviced.

Outbounds

Soon after coming to the RBI, Subbarao introduced the concept of outbounds for the senior management. In an outbound, the entire senior management, including the governor, all the deputy governors, the executive directors, heads of departments and regional directors, would go to a remote place and brainstorm on important issues relating to the organization that otherwise did not get much importance, given that central banking issues always took precedence. The nation's central bank was also very inward-looking and conscious of its public image. It is possible that, at a subconscious level, spending money on itself was perhaps not favoured. Subbarao pointed out that there was nothing wrong in spending some time and resources on self-improvement—as in, on the betterment of the organization. Moreover, the finance ministry used to already go for regular outbounds. And so the idea of outbound took off.

The outbound practice revealed a totally different side of the RBI officials. The days were packed with some team-building activities, some lecture sessions by eminent speakers and discussions on serious organizational issues. But the evenings were fun-filled. Some sang, some danced…and that included even the governor and deputy governors. I have an interesting anecdote to share here. As part of the team-building exercise, T-shirts with the RBI logo were given to all participants. We were supposed to wear them for the group photo session. All the women officers looked awful wearing the T-shirt on top of our saris. So, I casually remarked that the women in the team should be given saris or kurtas for the photo session. Surprisingly, the suggestion was implemented the very next year, and we received some elegant saris and kurtas from then on.

Once, I remarked that instead of sitting and deliberating only on serious topics, we could also sit together and watch a film or a play and analyse it. To my astonishment, the suggestion went through, and we saw a film together, followed by a discussion and analysis. It was, of course, a serious finance-related film. Nevertheless, a film alright. The outbounds started building some kind of camaraderie among the RBI officials. These meetings took a pause but have now restarted.

The Importance of Communication

Subbarao recognized the importance of communication and always made the Department of Communication a part of high-level meetings, including what we called the top-management meetings. Top-management meetings were those in which, apart from the governor, all the deputy governors and executive directors would participate. Involving the communication function in major decisions from the initial stages helped. Communication could be strategized and be proactive rather than reactive. During the global financial crisis, bankers' meetings were held almost every alternate day in the RBI and some communication would be issued after that to assure the markets. So, the communication function had to be present in all the meetings that discussed the crisis, its repercussions on the nation and the measures the central bank would be required to take. We often suggested strategies of communication at these meetings, which were implemented successfully. Involving the communication function in decision-making continued well into the next regime. But then it started tapering off and completely stopped.

Adding Stakeholders

Another very significant initiative in communication was taken in Subbarao's tenure. We started teleconferencing with researchers and analysts after each monetary policy was announced. This was an important category of the central bank's stakeholders that had grown over the years. It was important to reach out to them, as, with their specialist's viewpoint, they could mould public opinion, especially of the media and the foreign investors. And why not? Technology made it possible to communicate directly with them. The timing of the researchers' conference was carefully fixed—soon after the announcement of the policy—so that before they formulated and published their views, we could give them our perspective. This initiative drew good traction. In each conference, more than 300 participants would be listening in. Even other central banks wanted to emulate this initiative. It continued in Raghuram Rajan's time. Dr Urjit Patel also found it useful as many technical questions were raised at these interactions, and the answers provided clarity to the financial markets.

Subbarao also started the practice of the communication chief conducting the press conference, just as it should have been; this was already being done in other government institutions. This brought the Department of Communication closer to the governor in the seating arrangement of the press conference. Yes, prior to this, the seat of the press advisor in the press conference was at the end of the table. The norm in the RBI was that the department which organized a meeting would sit closest to the governor. But this privilege was never given to the Department of Communication. It was a press conference, yes, but on monetary policy. So the monetary policy department had that privilege and sat next to the governor. The issue was not so much of a privilege as of communication. If the governor wanted to communicate something to me during the press conference, he would have to really look for me in the room. But when Subbarao asked me to conduct the press conference, I took the opportunity and moved myself closer to the governor's seat, even if not next to him. This made things a bit easier, but not entirely.

In one press conference, I called upon a journalist by name to ask a question. The journalist was on the left in the row opposite the governor. Generally, I would also make a hand gesture so that the governor would be able to see that and turn to that side. But this time, he could not see me. I was sitting at the same table but on the sixth or seventh seat from him. The other officers who were sitting between us were blocking his view. So, when the journalist started asking his question, Subbarao looked to his right. This was embarrassing even if it was for a split second. And the journalist could have taken offence. Fortunately, that did not happen. In the next press conference, I tried to stand behind the governor. This, too, did not work as the governor still could not see me.

The primary issue wasn't resolved. It was resolved only in Rajan's time when we changed the venue and started organizing the press conference in the RBI's auditorium, where the top management sat on the stage and the media in the audience, like in a theatre. From then on, I would stand at the podium to conduct the conference, and so the governor could finally see me pointing at the audience and spot the journalist in time. Subbarao resisted the thought of doing the press conference in the auditorium. He found it too 'staged', perhaps.

Preps for the Media Interaction

By now, we had started announcing the monetary policy once every two months. With each policy announcement came the press conference and media interviews. We continued with the practice of giving interviews to financial newspapers and business channels. Subbarao would prepare extensively for the press conference as well as for the subsequent media interviews. All the departments involved in making the monetary and regulatory policies had to come up with questions relating to their functional areas and also answer them. The dossier so prepared would be discussed in a meeting, and modifications and nuances suggested. Communication contributed in making certain answers more nuanced in the context of how the matter was being covered in the media at that time. Once the dossier was finalized, the governor would go through it word by word and then articulate the responses in his own way in the press conference.

We also started using a teleprompter in Subbarao's time. In the first part of the press conference, Subbarao would read out the initial brief on the policy announcement, which we would webcast and the business channels telecast live for the world at large. By looking at the teleprompter, which ran the announcement on its screen, Subbarao would appear as if he was addressing the world. This, too, required practice, as the speed at which he read would have to match the speed of the person running the computer screen on the teleprompter. Subbarao would take time out from policy discussions to do this. For him, communication was as important as policy itself.

He prepared for media interviews separately. We would request the media to send their questions soon after the policy was announced but before the interview. The questions were sent to the respective departments. They would prepare answers, and the Department of Communication then rewrote them in understandable English. Interviews were quite an elaborate affair. We called all the financial media without discrimination—so, six financial newspapers and six financial news channels. Even if we gave the bare minimum time of 20 minutes to each of them, it took a day and a half to go through them all. Though it was absolutely exhausting, both Reddy and Subbarao never complained about it and did it as part of their job.

For the Department of Communication, this was quite an exercise. Interviews with six television channels would be held the day after the policy announcement. Getting questions from all the channels, getting the departments to prepare the answers and then editing and sending them to the governor, all had to be accomplished overnight. Subbarao would wake up at 4 a.m., read the answers and get ready for the interviews.

The Department of Communication worked the whole night to deliver the media questions along with their answers to the governor early in the morning and reported to duty as usual because the first interview would have been scheduled at around 9 a.m. To prevent the 'me first' competition in airing the interviews, we would embargo all the interviews for telecast till the last one was ready.

Working overnight was not a problem, but the way in which the departments functioned made delivery difficult for me. All the operational departments prepared a question bank for the press conference. We would ask the six financial media companies to share the questions in advance. The dossier was so exhaustive that the Department of Communication could have easily prepared responses to the media questions on its own by merely putting those answers in the perspective of the questions asked.

But this is a peculiarity in the RBI—protect your territory. Since this was monetary policy-related work, monetary policy department took upon itself the responsibility of coordinating the responses. So leave aside the policy, the questions and answers prepared for the press conference and the media would also be compiled by the monetary policy department and not the Department of Communication. Even the dossier prepared by the respective departments would not be shared with the Department of Communication—the nodal department for media.

In addition, each executive in charge of the department would have his or her own way of dealing with the subject. In this case, the head of the department insisted on sending the prepared responses to questions of all the six media channels together and not one by one as and when they were finalized. The result was that the Department of Communication would have to wait until dawn to receive the answers from the monetary policy department. Only then could I start working on them—turning those technically written responses into plain English and delivering the dossier to Subbarao at his residence so that he could prepare for the interview, all within an hour and a half.

I could deliver the responses only in the morning by 7–7.30 a.m. How Subbarao prepared after this is known only to him. The Department of Communication always wondered if it was a futile exercise. Perhaps not. Subbarao prepared hard. At the end of all the interviews, he would ask if anything needed to be changed or where and how he needed to improve. I would mumble something but nothing concrete, as I thought he was quite a pro at giving interviews. In the final exit interview that we—the house journal team and I—had organized before he took leave of the RBI, he told us that we did not point out his weaknesses during the preparation of media interviews. It was his wife, Urmila Subbarao, who did that. Urmila Madam, who was present at the exit interview, could only laugh. She said he rigorously practised in the morning in front of the mirror and corrected himself.

Brutal Honesty

All the governors had built a special rapport with the media during their tenure at the RBI and the media loved all of them equally. The media loved them because all of them were erudite, transparent and honest. Subbarao, in particular, was brutally honest. The editors' meeting, which we had started during Jalan's time and had continued in Reddy's time, was modified in format in Subbarao's time. He preferred a structured meeting with editors in which the agenda was set—either by the RBI or by the editors, preferably editors. Five topics were selected, the RBI outlined the issues on those topics one by one and then the discussion took place. It was a two-way street. Editors gave suggestions and opinions, and the RBI spoke freely about its approach.

The last such meeting before Subbarao's term was over was held in Delhi at my insistence. In this meeting he was so open and frank that he admitted that he had erred in not intervening in the foreign exchange market to check the rupee from rapid depreciation and had favoured conserving foreign exchange. The result was that the exchange rate of the rupee, which had been ₹55 to a dollar, fell to ₹65 to a dollar in a period of just nine months in 2013—the last year of his tenure as the RBI governor. The media had to tell him not to be so frank. 'After all, we are media,' they said. Such was the media's affection towards the RBI and its governors.

Most in the media brigade were young. Subbarao, even as the governor, was young at heart. Like other governors, when the time came to say goodbye, he agreed to ceremoniously say goodbye to the media as well. So, we invited the financial media to the governor's bungalow. There were food and drinks and music and song and dance. The media went crazy with excitement. They had not expected this. One, they were very excited to be invited to the governor's bungalow—a more-than-a-century-old heritage building. On top of that, it was an opportunity to interact with the governor informally—on non-central-banking issues. Subbarao also danced at the farewell party. That put the media at complete ease. I remember one journalist also got emotional and cried a bit, something that had never happened in any governor's farewell. The media, of course, was sworn to secrecy about the party. This was because, first, I was scared about getting calls the next day from the media persons who were not invited, and second, I did not want a page 3 coverage of the farewell of the RBI governor on his last day. And true to their word, not a single media person breached the promise.

Being a Commoner

With Subbarao, we were to see a new brigade of governors who did not like much chaperoning around them. Subbarao preferred to carry his own briefcase and luggage at the airport. He also did not like the offices spending on flowers to welcome him. His argument was that he was one of us, so why welcome him with flowers? Soon, the RBI gave up the *lal batti* (beacon lights) on the governor's car. Towards the end of his career in the RBI, Subbarao once told us that he would have loved to see Mumbai on his own without the security personnel around him. He also wanted to travel by a local train. And he did it!

On the very next day after his tenure ended, he took a train, got off at Bandra, went to Bandstand and came back. He told us that only one young student recognized him and took his autograph. He thought it was a small price to pay to do something that he had always wanted. He even visited a couple of pubs in Bandra to experience the pub culture of Mumbai. A television journalist spotted him in one of the pubs. But he was not bothered about it. To him, he was no longer the governor of the RBI and was not to be surrounded by security personnel.

The Battle Resurfaces

In his second term, the battle between the finance ministry and the RBI resurfaced. Reddy could swim through this, as he was not only an economist par excellence but also a master administrator. But for Subbarao, who had a doctorate in Economics with a thesis on fiscal reforms at the sub-national level, this was a little difficult. He was too straightforward for the wicked coterie—if it existed, that is. Whenever the finance ministry called for a meeting, he would take a detailed briefing from the RBI officials. This was a sea-change from his initial days in the RBI, when he would ask the RBI officials to simply listen to the bankers.

Many thought that during his tenure, the RBI lost much of its ground. The ministry appointed a board to select the bank chairpersons and even the deputy governors. The clamouring for separating the management of government's debt from the RBI became more vociferous. By the time Subbarao's tenure ended, the only major area left for the government to press openly upon was the audit of the RBI by the CAG of India. Had that happened, the RBI would have lost its functional autonomy.

While discharging its functions, the RBI takes decisions that may result in losses on the central bank's balance sheet. For instance, to preserve the value of the rupee, the RBI may intervene in the market and spend dollars at a rate lower than the rate at which it had bought them from the market. Or to prevent the market from charging the government very high interest rate on its bonds, the RBI buys the government securities from the market at a lower price than the market. These decisions are policy decisions and not commercial decisions, and can therefore not be questioned with hindsight as they are taken in the interest of the economy. There is always a fear that if the CAG starts auditing the RBI, its officers may not be able to take decisions in the interest of the economy. How can one explain a loss-making decision?

Among many such losses was the loss of Dr Subir Gokarn,

the deputy governor who was in charge of monetary policy and research. He was a fine economist and a finer person. Towards the end of Subbarao's tenure—he served for two tenures, the first one of three years and the next for two years—Gokarn's term was also coming to a close. Subbarao was pushing the government for the deputy governor's extension as he did not want any change at the fag end of his career. But, reportedly, the government was in no mood to listen. It was so angry about the RBI refusing to toe the line, that it decided to be vile about Gokarn. The government did not send any communication about Gokarn's extension till the last day, last hour. The RBI could not even plan his farewell, as everyone kept hoping for the extension till the last minute. But when no communication came till 5 p.m. on the last day of Gokarn's tenure, we at the RBI knew that he would have to go. Subbarao was indeed very pained at this behaviour of the government, and so was Gokarn. But nothing could be done about it.

At the next top-management meeting, Subbarao expressed his pain and said that this was because of his stand vis-à-vis the government. Gokarn's apparent fault was his speech a few months ago in which he admitted that India did not have adequate foreign exchange reserves to take on the market and preserve the value of the rupee. The market was waiting for some such signal at that time and the rupee took a severe beating in the market in the next few days. Reportedly, the government wanted him to pay the price for 'talking too much'. However, all this was market chatter and there was no way to confirm it. What was apparent and what we were witnessing was that Gokarn was ill-treated by the government. Subbarao, being the governor, could not have his say in choosing his own deputy governor, a privilege that governor after governor had been granted by the government so far. After this, a committee was instated for the selection of deputy governors, on which the RBI governor was a mere member and the government had the final say. One more battle with the government was lost.

It was also very clear by now that Subbarao himself would not get another term as governor. And a battle of words started between the governor and the finance ministry. Subbarao unreservedly expressed his opinions and virtually gave it back to the government. In fact, Subbarao's last year and a half in the RBI must have been quite painful for him. The relationship between the RBI and the government was deteriorating from sourness to bitterness. The government did not leave a single occasion to make a nasty remark against the RBI. After one monetary policy announcement, for example, when the RBI did not cut rates as the government had been expecting, the finance minister responded to a media query by quoting Rabindranath Tagore's 'Ekla Chalo Re (Walk Alone)'.[4]

Yet, in private, the relationship between the finance ministry and the RBI governors remained extremely cordial and respectful. At times, I wondered whether or not to believe the media's version of 'there is no smoke without fire', whether I was naive enough to believe what I saw and heard in the RBI and the briefing I often got.

Lobbying?

It was unfortunate that this animosity got carried into an international-meeting setting as well—a G20 meeting which was held in Mexico. These high-level meetings, involving finance ministers and central bank governors of all member

[4]Majumdar, Sourav, 'Ekla Chalo Re: Chidambaram Soldiers on Despite Challenges', *Firstpost*, https://tinyurl.com/yws8b6tx. Accessed on 30 October 2023.

countries, are arranged on a very large scale. The central bank deputy governors in charge of international affairs, along with the communication chiefs, would also be present. The RBI did not take its communication chief to such meetings. So, sitting in Mumbai, we used to arrange for interviews of the governor with foreign media. I kept pleading with Subbarao to take me along. I think, if left to decide on his own, he would have taken me along, but the RBI culture did not allow him to do so. For the RBI, monetary policy, economic research and bank regulation were the three main functions and all the rest were ancillary. The officials working in these departments walked around with their heads held an inch above others. Therefore, my accompanying the governor for those meetings seemed impossible. There was also a protocol to be followed. All central banks needed to send in advance the names and number of persons in the team that would attend the meetings at the G20 secretariat, and only those could attend the meetings whose names were cleared.

One day, Subir Gokarn, who was the deputy governor in charge of economic research and also the Department of Communication at that time, called me and asked me if I had a valid US visa on my passport. Fortunately, I did. He told me that the governor wanted me to go with the RBI team to Mexico where the G20 meetings were going to take place. Gokarn told me to be ready for travel. Perhaps there was scope to add one more name to the team this time, and my name was added at Subbarao's instruction. Next day, I got a confirmation from Gokarn that I was going to be a part of the team. That's how I travelled with the team to Mexico.

The meeting was a big jamboree. By way of preparation, I could do nothing due to my last-minute inclusion in the team. I did not know who of my counterparts from the other central banks were going. There was sheer chaos at the venue—or so it appeared to me, the one who was attending such a high-level international meeting of that scale for the first time. I completely depended on the veterans—the executive assistants of the governor and Gokarn—to lead me through the meetings. They attended these meetings every two months and knew exactly what was happening where. I just trudged along. The two interviews that I was supposed to coordinate happened as per schedule. But I didn't get to know much about the what and how of the meetings except for what the executive assistants told me.

What I learnt, though, was significant. Apparently, we had taken a particular stand at the meeting on some issue. When we tried to put forward that proposal, no one paid attention to it. Next day, China advocated for the same proposal and it was carried through with aplomb. I was told China had lobbied heavily to get the proposal through. Sad! Here was a so-called communication expert accompanying the India team but she did not know anything about the proposal, let alone lobby for it. We just did not think along those lines.

Not only the RBI, but even the government did not think on those lines. I learnt this the next day when the finance minister was supposed to arrive. There was a meeting between the governor and the deputy governor with their executive assistants to discuss and finalize the approach towards briefing the finance minister. The day went by and, as it turned out, the meeting did not happen and there was no briefing of the finance minister. I overheard someone from our team mention that the finance minister had no time slot available for the briefing. I felt sad. Was it just ego that prevented the finance minister from meeting the RBI governor and get an update about what had transpired in the meeting so far? Shouldn't the country's interests have taken an upper hand? I could only imagine what must have been happening at other similar meetings where the RBI might not even be involved. I could understand now why, despite all its advantages, India did not make it big at international forums.

Subbarao's Funny Bone

Subbarao had a wry sense of humour. In fact, he had a knack for using American phrases and kept up to date with the current usage. 'Smelling the coffee', 'knock on wood', 'cross the river by feeling the stones'… He loved to use such phrases in his speeches. He also liked to use humour in his speeches. In fact, I am yet to see someone who agonized so much over using humour. So much so that, on the one hand, the experts in the RBI prepared the core speech, on the other, we in the Department of Communication were asked to look for humorous or interesting anecdotes that he could use in the speech—generally in the opening or the closing part but also in between if they fitted well. At times, he even suggested using journalists to help out. The journalists, in response, would share anecdotes, and we had to see if any of those fitted in the speech. But sometimes a journalist would ask for an advance copy of the speech so that he could understand the context and insert an anecdote or humour at an appropriate place in the speech. Giving a speech in advance to the media was so far considered a heresy. But Subbarao understood the need, and we did sometimes share the speech in advance if it did not have any sensitive material.

Subbarao had, in fact, shown willingness to even pay the journalist for his contribution. In my view, however, journalists were only too willing to do something for the RBI and its governor, and I was quite sure they would not ask for any payment. They might have, though, asked for some favour, and that too a favour like getting access to the governor. This was easy to give and, therefore, we would seek help from a few trusted journalists to embellish the speech with humour.

One day, one senior journalist who was famous for his acerbic humour did ask me, 'What will I get in return?' This journalist was known in media circles for his greed. But even he, when asked what he would want, asked just for a meeting with the governor. That was easy with most governors, especially with a governor like Subbarao who was a seasoned IAS officer and media-savvy too. The meeting, though, was quite hilarious. I arranged for one, the journalist came, but then, for the first five minutes, there was no conversation. I could not make out if the journalist was intimidated and nervous or he did not expect me to be in that meeting. Or was he simply taking time to warm up?

Here is one more example of Subbarao's wry humour. Once, the late K.C. Chakraborty, who was the then RBI deputy governor and the chairman of SBI, got into a tiff on stage at a public function over the age-old subject of the RBI paying interest to banks on CRR. Now, CRR is the most effective way of sterilizing money as it compulsorily withdraws (impounds) money from the banking system and locks it up on the RBI balance sheet. This created a dent in their balance sheets, which meant that banks paid the price for government's fiscal profligacy. Banks kept demanding interest on the CRR that was kept with the RBI as compensation. From the balance-sheet angle, the bankers were well-justified in asking the RBI to pay interest on CRR. But for the RBI, paying interest on CRR meant negating the action taken by increasing CRR. By increasing CRR, if the RBI was trying to immobilize some liquidity from the system by paying interest on it, it was putting some money back into the system, thus negating its own step of sucking out liquidity.

This had been going on since Rangarajan's time. But by the time Reddy left the RBI, this issue had settled. Reddy had got the Reserve Bank of India Act amended, and now, under the act, the RBI could not pay interest on CRR. Yet, the SBI chairman, in an open forum, had asked the RBI to consider paying interest on CRR. The late K.C. Chakraborty, who was known for his plainspeak, had argued vehemently with him from the same platform. The public had had a hearty laugh at this. Subbarao, who was speaking at the same forum a day later, had to make good for that public showdown. So he started with a joke, which was in any case his usual style. He said he would set up a committee…and then he took a short pause. By this time, reporters who were present at the event rushed out to file the headlines. Fortunately, before they shot out the headline, he completed his sentence, saying he would lock the concerned chairman and the concerned deputy governor in a room till they resolved their differences. The entire matter turned into a big joke and the media, too, reported it as an aside rather than as a serious difference of opinion between banks and the RBI. Here was a lesson in communication about setting a conflict at naught.

On the Wrong Side

In the RBI, freedom of speech was always valued. Even the junior-most staff members could express their point of view freely in the notes that were put up for consideration on policy issues. Any disagreement on the views was also recorded on this note. Thus, the top management could see both sides of any policy issue while reading the notes. However, as a disciplined bureaucracy, once a decision was taken, the entire hierarchy would defend that decision irrespective of the individual viewpoint.

Chakraborty once got on the wrong side of the management on an issue. The RBI was on the verge of hiking interest rates but, at that policy, it did not raise the rates. It was very common for the media at that time to picket at the gates of the finance ministry and catch hold of all visitors of the finance ministry, especially the RBI governor and deputy governors, to get a sound bite. The hot topic always was which way would the interest rates move? Soon after the policy announcement, Chakraborty happened to visit the finance ministry. That's where the media caught hold of him and asked him about the interest rates. He was perhaps of the view that the RBI should have raised the interest rate in that policy. So, he spoke his mind. He, perhaps, did not have his guard up and also used some unparliamentary language. The media did not report the language, but his counterview went as a big headline on wire agencies. To be fair to the media, knowing the sensitivity of the matter, the media did not quote Chakraborty by name, but everyone knew who was being quoted. I was summoned by the governor to get the name of the official being quoted and what exactly he had said. The media, due to our cordial relationship, not only confirmed to me that it was indeed Chakraborty but also told me what exactly had he said. Naturally, the governor and the other deputy governors decided to take action against him. He was divested of all his portfolios, barring only a couple of insignificant ones. This was perhaps for the first time in the history of the RBI that such an action was taken against a high-level official.

I suggested we issue a press release as usual about the

change in portfolios of deputy governors so that the media would not fly kites about it. So, we announced the changes on the RBI's website. The next day, the press wrote about how the deputy governor had been punished by divesting him of all his portfolios. To the credit of Chakraborty, he did not run away from the scene by resigning. He, of course, got all his portfolios back in a few months. There were editorials in the media discussing if the action taken by the RBI was correct.

The point is simple. In a bureaucratic organization, which the RBI is, one has all the opportunities to express one's point of view when the issues are being discussed. But once a decision was taken after considering all points of view, one is expected to justify the stand taken and not express a divergent view publicly, especially in a matter like interest rates, as divergent views on interest rates can vitiate the financial markets. The management thought it was necessary to make it known to all concerned that dissenting publicly on issues such as interest rates would not be tolerated.

Thank God It Exists...

There was a typical way in which the government and the RBI fought with each other. While the government invariably used the media to get to the RBI, the RBI got back to the government through the speeches made by its top executives—normally the governor himself or one of the deputy governors—at some public forum. And invitations for the RBI governor to give a public speech were aplenty. Like Jalan, Subbarao also delivered his last speech as the governor in Mumbai. He closed the chapter of his governorship with the now famous quote, saying, 'A final thought on this issue of autonomy and accountability. There has been a lot of media coverage on policy differences between the government and the RBI. Gerard Schroeder, the former German Chancellor, once said, "I am often frustrated by the the Bundesbank. But thank God, it exists." I do hope Finance Minister Chidambaram will one day say, "I am often frustrated by the RBI, so frustrated that I want to go for a walk, even if I have to walk alone. But thank God, the RBI exists.'"

Succession-Planning at the Top?

Still, good things kept happening. Before his tenure ended, Subbarao, in a way, paid back the kindness that he had received from his predecessor. At the end of his tenure, Reddy had taken upon himself to announce that the government had rejected the pension upgradation for RBI employees. When this happened, it had been decided that Reddy was leaving the RBI and Subbarao was going to take over. So, the announcement could have been either the final announcement by Reddy or the opening announcement for Subbarao. Apparently, Reddy took it upon himself to share the bad news before leaving, rather than getting Subbarao to open his account with such an announcement and create ill-will among the RBI employees.

The successor to Subbarao had already been announced—Raghuram Rajan. There were still some months to go for Subbarao. It had never happened in the history of the RBI that a successive governor was appointed almost six months in advance. Was this succession being planned at the top or was it some kind of a message to the incumbent governor? Media interpreted this as the government imposing Rajan on Subbarao just to slight him. Subbarao, though, told us that he himself had requested the government to appoint a successor ahead of time as an understudy of sorts while he was still holding the office so that he could induct him well into the job. This was a good corporate governance practice, he would tell us. Some said this was a face-saving tactic he might have adopted, but he sincerely utilized these months to show the ropes to Rajan. That was magnanimity indeed on his part.

As part of his induction, Rajan came and met many of us. He had already started working on taking the brewing foreign exchange crisis head-on once he took over. But more about that in the next chapter.

Penance?

Like all the RBI employees, the governors, too, got a last leave fare concession—an allowance to travel anywhere in India before retirement. Subbarao went to the last point in eastern India and took a train from there to Kanyakumari in the south with his wife. He travelled second class throughout. He was the harshest critic of himself. Did he think what he had got so far in life was undeserved? I had asked him so in his exit interview. His answer was affirmative. I wonder till today if I read too much into his reply.

6

Raghuram Rajan

Only Tall, Dark and Handsome?

Being tall, dark, handsome and young, Dr Raghuram Rajan (in office: 2013–2016) was already a heartthrob of the Delhi media, who he had already interacted with while serving the government as its chief economic advisor. It was Manmohan Singh who, while being the finance minister, had invited Indian economists serving abroad to come and work in India. Everyone knew that the chief economic advisor's post was only a back-stop arrangement for Rajan and that one day he would become the RBI governor. I did not believe in this. All the RBI governors so far had been well past their 60s. How could someone who was not even 50 become the RBI governor? So when his name was announced as the twenty-third governor of the Reserve Bank of India, no one was surprised but me!

Media in Mumbai, especially the young female reporters, went berserk and called me up, requesting for his interview. The young girls started following the RBI beat only so that, one day, they could come and interview this tall, dark, handsome Mills & Boon hero who happened to be the RBI governor.

A Warm Welcome

On the day Rajan was to take over as the governor, we had, as usual, arranged for a photo opportunity for the media. By now, making the new governor walk the ramp had settled down as a normal practice, cameras lined up on the ramp of the RBI building. The excitement to see the new governor was pulsating in the media as well as in the RBI fraternity.

Media had gathered on the ramp in large numbers, so we pushed all RBI employees into the waiting area of the building. Fortunately, the waiting area of the building was very large. However, it, too, was filled with people who had gathered to see the new governor. Rajan walked the ramp and entered the waiting area of the RBI building. He stopped for a split second and saw the huge crowd.

I wonder what must have gone through his mind at that time. It was an awkward moment for sure. He perhaps wanted to wait a minute and acknowledge the presence of the RBI employees. But the enormity of the crowd and the uncertainty about the protocol must have made him hesitate in doing what he wanted to do. So, after that momentary pause, he walked along with his head down. The crowd suddenly broke into a spontaneous applause. As it was an enclosed area, the acoustics made for an absolutely theatrical resounding applause. This was overwhelming. Even Rajan would not have expected this kind of welcome, I am sure. Ironically, in this very area of the building, we would do an open house for him some three years down the line before he would leave the RBI—an exercise we had started to enable the *aam* (common) RBI employee to interact with the governor. But more about it later.

A Financial Economist

The RBI fraternity, especially the economist type, was not too enamoured by Governor Rajan. For such economists in the RBI, he was not an economist—at least not of the RBI kind.

Rajan was a financial economist. The typical RBI economist is almost invariably a monetary economist and a purist who believes that monetary policy is only about money, and that the central bank should only focus on monetary policy and no other function. Among all RBI governors during my tenure, only Rangarajan had been a monetary economist so far.

If not a monetary economist, even someone as high-up as a governor may not be able to draw enough respect from a blue-blooded RBIite. This should, however, not be mixed up with the respect for the governor's chair. A typical RBI employee would have the utmost respect for the chair of the governor, and would, like a good soldier, carry out every order coming out of the governor's office with the utmost care and caution. They would justify just about any policy once they were convinced about the policy or that the 'chair' required it. What would lack is the awe for the person.

Setting up the Agenda...

Not being a monetary economist hardly affected Rajan's work in the RBI. The time given to him by Subbarao for briefing gave him an insight into the RBI's functioning and the issues it faced. The foreign exchange crisis had already been staring in the RBI's face when his name was announced as the next RBI governor. Soon, he started working on this crisis, and by the time he took charge as the governor, he had drawn up a list of five tasks that he wanted to undertake during his tenure.

Then there was the issue of the NPAs. He wanted to take the bull by the horns and, even before joining the RBI, had worked on several solutions for NPAs. He clearly outlined his five-point agenda in his opening statement for the world outside.[5] As he narrated his agenda to us in the senior management committee, my first reaction was to communicate it in some manner to the world outside. He agreed to make a statement, but the monetary policy had already been scheduled, which was to be announced in a couple of days after he took over as the governor. The dilemma was whether Rajan should make the statement on the agenda a day before the policy announcement or if he should announce it as a part of the policy. Announcing the agenda a day before would make the market read policy in it, and announcing it as part of the policy would take away the punch from the policy. From the viewpoint of communication, both the statement on the agenda and Rajan's first policy were equally significant.

After much discussion, we ultimately decided to postpone the monetary policy announcement and to go with Rajan making a statement about his agenda in a press conference in the evening of his taking over. He wrote out a statement, as he would do for all his statements and speeches going forward. Transparency and predictability were going to be the two guiding principles, he said in his statement; and so, from day one, clear and constant communication prevailed during Rajan's tenure.

Many significant initiatives were undertaken during Rajan's tenure. Apart from stabilizing the exchange rate after the 'Taper Tantrum' and restoring confidence in the rupee by building foreign exchange reserves from the low they had reached by raising deposits from NRIs (non-resident Indians), bringing down inflation from near double digits to the target range,

---

[5]Reserve Bank of India, 'Statement by Dr. Raghuram Rajan on Taking Office on September 4, 2013', 4 September 2013, http://tinyurl.com/y37ud8my. Accessed on 18 February 2024.

and signing an accord with the government to implement the inflation-targeting framework, along with setting up the monetary policy committee, were the major steps taken in the monetary policy space.

After freeing branch banking and licensing nearly 20 banks of different kinds (including new small finance banks and payment banks), the RBI put bank licensing on tap. The beginnings of UPI (Unified Payments Interface), TReDS (Trade Receivables electronic Discounting System) and Bharat Bill Pay were also made in Rajan's time. Each development was clearly communicated to the media proactively and upfront, which helped a great deal in getting the RBI's viewpoint across before the opinions of commentators started to colour the external world's view.

As if this agenda was not enough, he undertook reform within the RBI too. Which agenda was more challenging, it was difficult to say—external or internal?

...But Hold On

As he was coming to grips with hardcore central banking issues, we had to deal with some smaller issues from the communication angle. The first issue was his familiarity with the Delhi media. We organized his first press conference to announce the tasks he had listed out for himself. A lady reporter from Delhi media, who was quite influential, insisted on meeting him for an interview. Rajan didn't want to start with the media interviews just yet. Since most Delhi media had Rajan's mobile number, they would ring him directly and it would be difficult for him to say no. This, in fact, was a problem with all executives in the RBI. No one wanted to be unpopular by saying no. She would keep calling Rajan and he, in turn, would tell me to keep the journalist at bay. But the journalist would not give up. At one point, he told me point-blank, 'Can you not deal with her?' My answer was very clear. For me to deal with her, he had to give up dealing with her! He understood my point and asked me to deal with her. Only then could I make the lady reporter understand that, in the RBI, we followed certain rules that we believed were fair to the media as well as to us. She also understood and backed off. The reporter and I later became good friends. I have always believed that if you explained your stand to the media, they would understand and appreciate it.

Image Makeover

The second issue we had to deal with as soon as Rajan joined the RBI was his image. When he took over as the governor, one celebrity author wrote a piece on him in the country's leading financial newspaper. She had called him 'James Bond', punning on the word 'bond'. The image published with that write-up showed Rajan as James Bond in a Bond-like action. In the article, the columnist had said that 'the guy's put "sex" back into the limp sensex'. This was embarrassing. I asked the governor if he was okay with that kind of coverage. He emphatically said he was not. 'I have a wife and a young daughter,' he said and asked me to change that image if I could.

For the next few months, we gave photographs taken by us to the media and did not allow any media person to photograph him unless he was on a public platform. Photos clicked on a public platform were not a concern as, while making a speech in public, he would stand against a lectern and wear his reading glasses on his nose. This gave him a professorial look, which was the image we wanted to settle with in the media. Later, the bespectacled photograph of Rajan became the norm. His height gave him a certain appeal that would detract from the image of an RBI governor that we wanted for him. So, I had to control his photography sessions with the media and the way he would pose in those sessions.

Is image important for an institution like the RBI and its governor? I would say yes, because an institution like the RBI, which does not deal directly with the public, has to have credibility and trust. Most people do not read, follow or understand what the RBI does, but they intuitively trust this institution and believe that its actions are in their interest and benefit. And so, the RBI must have an image in the public eye that is trustworthy. I remember a lady acquaintance once telling me to change a certain governor's photo that routinely appeared in the media. I asked her why, and she told me that the photo did not inspire confidence!

Citizenship Muddle

When Rajan came in as the governor from Delhi, a controversy followed him—his citizenship. A politician kept instigating the media regarding Rajan's rumoured US citizenship. Every other day, this would get mentioned in some newspaper or the other.[6] He got quite fed up with this and asked me if there was a way to put this issue to rest. Before suggesting any way, I asked him if there was any truth in it. His answer was an emphatic no. He had a green card and had never even applied for US citizenship, he told me. The press conference that followed the announcement of every monetary policy was on the anvil at that time. So I told him that I would get a question asked

---

[6]PTI, 'Raghuram Rajan Taken Aback by Query About Citizenship', *The Times of India*, 29 October 2013.

on his citizenship at the presser and he should answer that question in a straightforward manner. He agreed.

Now I had to look for a journalist who was trustworthy and would look credible in asking that question. I could have asked anyone from the Mumbai brigade to ask that question and I knew I could trust them. But that question coming from a journalist in Mumbai would not look credible. So I set my eyes on the Delhi media. There was this young journalist, quite sincere and very respectful of the RBI. He covered economy and finance ministry from Delhi for one of the largest circulated newspapers. I took him into confidence; after some reluctance, he agreed to ask the question. Going by his hesitation, I wondered to myself if I should have kept a backup ready, just in case he didn't ask that question. But I didn't. The press conference was progressing, and the journalist was showing no sign of asking any question, leave aside the desired question. I started worrying. We almost came to the close of the conference, when I saw him raise his hand. Since I conducted these conferences, I immediately gave him the opportunity. He started by asking a question about the policy. Once again, I got worried. He then slipped that question on citizenship almost under his breath. Thankfully, the governor was alert. He caught the question and answered in unequivocal terms that he did not have a foreign passport or citizenship and that he had never applied for one. And the controversy was given a decent burial. I, naturally, was grateful to that journalist, who remains a friend even today.

Media by Our Side

The external agenda—mainly the NPAs—was a huge challenge too. Only estimating them accurately took one full year. For the first time, the RBI simultaneously checked loan accounts of a certain size across banks. And that gave the real picture of the NPAs. Rajan had worked out several approaches to deal with NPAs, with the ultimate aim of making the borrowers pay up. The solutions were complex and needed to be explained well. It was important to have the media on our side on this issue. So, I suggested that we do an informal briefing of the media to explain the objective of the approaches. The governor immediately agreed, and we called the media. To my surprise, Rajan himself was present to explain the solutions. This was an unexpected bonanza for the media and had the desired effect. We received good support from the media in news reporting as well as in the editorials. Of course, with the governor himself explaining the issue, we could not keep the briefing off-the-record. So we had to let the media quote Rajan—not by name, though—for some of the explanations. It was a small compromise for what it allowed us to achieve.

Interacting with Gen Z

We could and did take several new initiatives in communication in Rajan's time. Being a professor, he loved to talk to the student community and explain concepts to them. He obviously was a great speaker and connected with students instantly. The first such request came from a students edition of a leading newspaper. I hesitatingly asked the governor if he would like to speak with students. He readily agreed. These were school children studying in Classes 8 to 10. The hall was brimming with students and the session was a roaring success.

The questions the students asked were essentially simple yet difficult at times to answer. But Rajan was in his element here and responded to each question with élan. For instance, one Class 8 student asked him, 'When will we see the day when fluctuations in the value of the rupee would affect the whole world?' The seemingly easy question was challenging to explain. Rajan took a deep breath, appreciated the question and replied. Roughly put, he said, the RBI was putting in place policies so as to maintain the value of the rupee with the currencies of the world. It might not happen in his time, but in the lifetime of the student who asked this question, this could happen, he added. That was a clincher. The question and the answer both received a thumping applause. The next day, we learnt that the question and the answer both had gone viral on social media and the student had become an overnight celebrity. After this, we had to put restrictions on putting such interactions on social media. The problem was, if quoted out of context, the responses coming from the RBI governor could move the markets. Not that the ban worked, but we learnt a lesson about the power of social media and tried closing a gap.

After the session, it was selfie time, the audience being of the selfie generation. The students started moving onto the stage. The hosts got worried. They told me that if many students rushed onto the stage, it might just give way. I had to think on my feet. I went to the stage and announced that no student was to come to the stage for a selfie but that the governor would go to them for it. I requested Rajan to go and stand amidst the students so that we could take the selfie for them. A classic case of the Mountain going to Mohammed! But with Rajan, this was easy. He understood the young generation well and had no inhibitions or airs of being an important public personality. The first session with the youth had rocked, which opened a floodgate of invites. Soon, we had to become selective.

The interaction with students started happening more frequently. Interviews with media did not come through easily, but invitations for interacting with students and giving speeches were easy to get through with Rajan. In fact, interactions would often replace a request for an interview at my prompting. I would request the media, especially the television channels, to tie up with a college or a university for a student interaction and record the event for telecast. The interactions served the purpose of familiarizing the student community with the economy and the functions of the RBI, and lent themselves less to controversies. At the same time, the interaction could be in the public domain rather than remaining confined to a particular college or university. We found a new way to explain the RBI's role and functions to the general public—interactions with the student community.

Using Social Media

'Context' is a very important factor for central bank communication. Quoted out of context, which the media often does, statements from the central banks can play havoc with the markets. Since the format of communication on social media also requires one to be brief, central banks the world over were initially not too keen on using this medium. In fact, many central banks had registered their presence on social media and had later withdrawn. They would not even monitor what was being said about them on social media. Yet, I did not want to miss the opportunity, knowing a new-age governor like Rajan would be willing to experiment. However, given the experience of other central banks, we had to start cautiously. We began with X (formerly Twitter) first. That, too, was automated. Whatever was published on the RBI's website, the headline of that communication would automatically get tweeted. Today, in addition to X, the RBI quite successfully uses social media—Instagram, LinkedIn and Facebook—to spread financial awareness among the younger generation.

Speeches

Rajan would very carefully choose the venue and the subject for a speech. He would write his own speeches. This was new for us. The previous governors got the RBI staff to write draft speeches—some of them, especially Reddy, covering the entire history of the topic on which they were to speak. They would review the draft prepared by the staff, give additional points and nuances and then rewrite that draft in their own style. Subbarao liked to brainstorm in detail, right from the subject of the speech to its title and the content; he would then rewrite the final speech or get one of us to rewrite it.

Like most governors, Rajan, too, sent the drafts to me, and to some other officers in the RBI, for feedback. We would ruthlessly but politely point out problem areas in the speech—words, sentences or thoughts that the media would pick up to create controversy. He would invariably change those phrases or explain them further, if necessary, so that they were understood as he wanted to express them. Yet, the media would twist and turn phrases to create unpleasant controversies.

Once, he sent to me the draft of a particular speech he was going to deliver in Delhi. There were just a couple of days left before the event. I thought the speech was explosive as he had chosen examples that were in the news. Given the milieu that prevailed around that time, I was quite sure those examples would be completely misunderstood or misinterpreted. So I pointed that out in my comments, highlighting the phrases and words that could be misunderstood or misinterpreted. I even suggested, a bit hesitatingly though, that he should replace those examples with examples revolving around economics or central banking. That was tantamount to rewriting virtually the entire speech. I thought he would not rewrite it. There was also very little time to make such a drastic change in the speech. To my utter surprise, the next day another draft got dropped in my email inbox. He had replaced all the examples that I had pointed out with those from economics or central banking, as I had suggested. Even though some of the controversial thoughts and phrases still remained, he had rewritten the entire speech overnight.

Unfortunately, despite this hard work, we could not escape controversy as the media caught onto some of the words and phrases that had remained in the speech and played them up. Later, I asked him out of curiosity why he had to comment on the controversial issues. Rajan was bold and never shirked from taking a stand on issues, even though media, more often than not, reported his statements out of context and even coloured them to make them controversial. 'With my background and status, if I don't take a stand, who will?' was his candid and earnest reply. True! If no one spoke, how would things change? Rajan believed in bringing about change that was needed—be it in the RBI or in policymaking. What he lacked, perhaps, was political acumen.

Pampering the Youngsters

Rajan was perhaps the only governor during my tenure who dared to bring about a change in the RBI internally. Having been trained and having worked in the West, he was not used to hierarchy. He would call people by their first names and expect them to call him 'Raghu', as he was known in his circle. People in the RBI were not used to this yet. So they called him governor in public and perhaps called him by his name when they met him one-on-one. He would walk into the cabin of any deputy governor or executive director; that gradually extended to department heads' cabins. He would chat freely with the staff of the departments he visited. He loved to talk to youngsters, in the organization and outside. He slowly turned visiting the departments into a practice. These visits were supposed to be a surprise for the departments. But in the RBI, we found it difficult to accept that a governor would walk down to a department and meet young junior officers. So, on the pretext of maintaining security protocol, his security officer would alert the department head ahead of Rajan's visit. And soon, it became an organized event, defeating the very purpose for which he had started the activity.

One day, Rajan landed up in the 'lounge' at lunch time, to have lunch with the young officers of the RBI. The RBI has a full-fledged food service for its employees. For officers, it is in a space called the 'lounge'. The lunch there is quite elaborate—from soup till dessert. There is also a 'canteen', which is for the non-officer staff, which also serves full meals, and quite delicious ones at that; many officers regularly ate at the canteen. But Rajan started his meal-visits with the lounge. The food served at a concessional rate in the lounge is cooked in-house. There is a whole category of staff that works in the RBI kitchen. At one point in time, there used to be a category called *khansama*, an Urdu word for a male chef, which was later abolished. Most of the staff in the RBI would eat in the lounge or the canteen and, hence, these spaces used to be more or less packed during lunch hours. Rajan wanted to connect with the young employees and have unstructured discussions with them on general issues concerning them, mainly their career progression and development. He would meet them under any excuse and encourage them to talk. His lounge visits became fairly regular—almost once every week—but were unannounced. And young officers just loved this practice.

By this time, the profile of the RBI staff had changed quite a bit. There had been voluntary retirements twice, and many young people were recruited. Earlier, all recruits had to do a stint in the currency department of the RBI in the initial few years of their career. The currency function is the core function of the RBI, besides monetary policy. The currency department and regional offices were places where one could experience the real RBI. The RBI of yore was a staff-heavy institution—approximately 60,000 employees in the early 1990s, largely class III and IV, meaning clerks and peons. One learnt people management only in the currency department and in regional offices. A stint in these areas was, therefore, a must before one could get into senior management. Currency management, though, was among the unglamorous functions. Regulatory and supervisory departments and departments that manage government's debt, foreign exchange reserves or financial markets were the departments where the young generation wanted to be posted. And why not? They were well qualified—most of them being engineers, chartered accountants or MBAs. So, when the governor would meet them informally in the lounge, they vehemently argued for being posted to those glamorous departments and cribbed if they were posted to regional offices or currency departments. Rajan always listened to them patiently, and would try to find a balance between keeping the young motivated and maintaining the organizational requirement of moving the staff around to give them varied experience. Retaining the young employees was important, as the RBI did need fresh blood.

RBI as an Expert Organization

Among the many initiatives that Rajan took in the RBI, developing domain expertise was a significant one. In Reddy's time, we did initiate setting up a research-cum-training establishment aimed at ultimately taking the RBI's training capacity to other central banks, especially in the neighbouring countries. This effort fructified as CAFRAL (Centre for Advanced Financial Research and Learning) in Subbarao's time, with Manmohan Singh inaugurating it as the prime minister.

The norm of periodically transferring officers had, perhaps, resulted in having a large number of 'jack of all trades' in the RBI and very few masters. Rajan wished to change this. He was prompted to do this by senior officers who, in two presentations made by two separate groups at a senior management conference, presented the same idea—of developing cadres—cadres of bank regulators and supervisors, market professionals and even currency managers. There was also a suggestion of the merging of two separate streams in the RBI—economists and statisticians with generalists. The non-economist category was known as generalists, as these people did not fall in the category of 'specialists' or economists.

Rajan favoured specialization. The RBI perhaps believed in generalization. The generalist staff was transferred among various departments and offices every three to five years. This meant that, by and large, no one developed expertise in any subject. In the very first senior management meeting after Rajan took charge as governor, two senior management groups suggested the restructuring of the RBI. This included reorganizing departments to functionally streamline them and suitably align the role of the deputy governors. Earlier, we had separate regulatory and supervisory functions for commercial banks, co-operative banks and NBFCs. So a supervisory circular would be issued for the commercial banks and a few days later, the same circular would be issued by another department for the co-operative banks. Rajan took the bull by the horns and appointed committees to chalk out the streamlining of the departments and functions. Strategically, the committees headed by executive directors comprised senior management of the RBI. This was to ensure that the restructuring finalized by these committees would be acceptable to the staff. The recommendations of these committees were further discussed by the management committee, consisting of the governor, deputy governors and executive directors. The final version that emerged was thus a consensus plan which was released into the system for implementation.

Economists took pride in the fact that the RBI exists because *they* exist. For them, it was the economists who gave credibility to the institution. This came from monetarists, according to whom the central bank should only make monetary policy and operationalize it. Banking regulation and supervision, and the rest of the functions, were an adjunct role for the central bank. The economists, it seemed, would look down upon the generalists. Yes, they indeed were called generalists and not bank regulators, bank supervisors or currency managers. I have no idea who created these categories and why. But they existed.

That cross-breeding would bring only enrichment to both sides was somehow never recognized. So economists kept researching in isolation with little idea of how research worked in real banking situations, while generalists kept analysing operational issues without much background in economic theories or research models. Generalists did not even undertake operational research in their functional areas. Deputing at least one economist from the economic research department to operational departments had perhaps started when Reddy was the governor. But, unfortunately, their deployment in operational departments was seen as a means to create more posts for the economists, and was, therefore, never welcomed by the generalists. They were just ignored. Even the economic research department did not try to post its best talent in operational departments, implying indispensability in the home department.

Communication: A Strategic Function

When Rajan undertook reorganization of the RBI, communication was not a part of the plan, though I, as an officer, was aware of these developments. The initiative met with a serious backlash. The cadres revolted, instigated slyly by some in the top management.

The top management—some of them—also did not like the communication function being a part of decision-making, even if it was for just listening in and contributing only from a communication angle. Listening to the discussions leading to a particular decision enabled me to think of strategic communication. Many, unfortunately, believed that communication was only a residual function and not strategic, and so should come only at the end to just get what was to be communicated to the outside world. This weakened my hold over thinking strategically for communication, and most of the time, I could not brief the media proactively.

At the functional level, though, I was completely in command. By now, I even had a WhatsApp group with the media, through which we used to communicate mundane as well as important things. The governor knew about the group. Once, we were announcing a major decision on the foreign exchange regulation front. The regulation was complex and significant. I had worked on the press release, so I knew about it. I was pushing the concerned department to give me the press release at the latest by 5 p.m. But as always, the deadline kept extending. I had alerted the media already, so the media was pushing me to bring it out quickly. At one point, the governor called me on my internal phone to ask if the communication was out. I said in jest, 'Where is it?', meaning I was still awaiting the document to come from the department. He then realized that the department was going to take its own time to release it. So he asked me to use my WhatsApp group and do something.

I sent the draft notification as well as the draft press release on the group with a strict embargo and told the media to keep their stories ready. They could release their headlines and stories only when both were published on the RBI website. This helped the media to understand a complex regulation well and write sensibly about it. They could even ask me a couple of questions before writing, for better clarity. The episode only demonstrated that giving more time to the media worked in our favour and keeping the person in charge of communication in the loop helped improve communication.

In that sense, I was lucky. Venkitaramanan, my first governor, called me into meetings as and when he remembered and when it was possible to involve me. Tarapore understood this need well and, to begin with, he gave me a seat at the bankers' meeting with the governor in which he announced the monetary policy. Jalan was a communicator par excellence and used communication proactively. But it was during Subbarao's tenure that communication got a seat—well almost—in top-management meetings. Initially, it started because of the platinum jubilee celebrations. Communication was the most important element of the celebrations. As communication became part of the top-management meetings, I was invited to those even when other issues were being discussed, helping me understand the issues better and also think of strategic communication.

Unknown to me, however, there were undercurrents working against me, and slowly I stopped getting those invites. I never lost an opportunity to stress upon involving communication early on in decision-making. Rajan kept promising me that he would restart the practice of inviting the communication department to such meetings at an opportune time. Alas! That never happened and communication again got relegated to a residual function. But not before giving me one more opportunity to reiterate my belief.

Internal Communication

Rajan's efforts to reorganize the institution displeased a whole lot internally. He also brought an economist from outside and put her in the regular employment of the RBI at a very senior level, overriding many an aspirant. The regular RBI cadres did not take this lying down—so to say. I kept on giving leads to him on how to communicate his stand internally whenever I had the opportunity. He did use those leads, I could see. But the distance between the communication department and the top management kept increasing. One day, a newspaper came up with a report about the internal simmer. I remember, it was a holiday and, early in the morning, the governor called me up. He was upset with me for not managing the media well on the internal bickering. I thought this was my opportunity, and I indignantly asked him how I could have managed the media when I had no brief! The conversation led to at least ten suggestions from my side about how we could bring the situation under control. He listened. At the end he said, 'Okay. All of them approved. Now get going.' So I embarked on a communication exercise which included internal communication.

The RBI undertook a massive outreach campaign within the organization. The Department of Communication, which so far did only external communication, spearheaded this exercise in internal communication. The communication was termed 'Town Hall'. Town hall meetings or town halls are usually a way for local and national politicians to meet with their constituents to hear them out. In recent times, youth icons, such as the erstwhile US President Barack Obama, have done town halls. Rajan made himself available to all staff in these events and responded to their questions and concerns, mainly relating to human resources. He dealt with the employees' concerns quite frankly and honestly. We started grabbing any opportunity for such communication that came our way. When the governor visited regional offices, we did a town hall there. By the end of Rajan's journey in the RBI, which was quite abrupt, the disgruntled employee sentiment had mellowed significantly. It was a good initiative and served well at that time, fulfilling the purpose for which it was undertaken. That communication never got its seat at the table was sad, but what could one do about the management decision anyway!

The Exit

For most of us, Rajan's exit from the RBI came suddenly. He decided to leave at the end of his tenure. However, he announced his exit almost four months earlier. He wrote a letter to the RBI employees to convey his decision. After discussion, we decided to place the letter on the RBI's website with a covering note, as the financial markets would react to such an important announcement. Media speculated that Rajan brought his early exit upon himself by criticizing the incumbent government incessantly on various issues, including those which did not fall under the RBI's purview. That a person of Rajan's stature took a stand in public on important issues did not matter to them as they seemed to have a different agenda. He had created too many adversaries, or so it seemed. Political leaders, bankers and even industrialists—all of whom felt the noose tightening around their necks for repaying their bank loans—some of them were made to repay their loans.

While one will never find out what made him go, what he himself told us was that the government wanted to give him another three years' term but he wanted only six months to complete his agenda of cleaning up the banks' balance sheets. He was keen to be with his family in the US as his son was soon to start college and he did not want to miss out on his growing years, he told us. A tug of war between six months and three years created a stalemate. Dialogues between the government and Rajan continued till June 2016. Rajan, however, could not wait indefinitely for the government to decide. To go back to academics, he needed to convey his decision to the university well in time for them to schedule his sessions. So, in June 2016, Rajan announced his decision to go back to academics after completing his term, and left in September when his term ended. The government did not stop him from going.

The Legacy

Rajan may have had his skirmishes with the government but he had a lot of regard for the RBI as an institution. When Urjit Patel was to take over from him as the next governor, Rajan presented him with a memento. It was the rupee symbol made of metal. While handing it to Patel, he told him that every governor of the RBI has had to face some crisis or the other on the Rupee. And it was the governor's job to preserve its value—internal (inflation) and external (exchange rate). So, a Rupee symbol was an ideal memento to be passed on from the outgoing governor to the incoming governor, he had said. What Patel ended up facing in his tenure was, ironically, demonetization! I am not sure if the memento is still kept in the governor's office or if it is in the Secretary's Department where all gifts and presents received by the governors are preserved.

An old wise man—a bureaucrat and a former central banker—had once advised Rajan to choose a deputy governor from the IAS when the post of one deputy governor fell vacant. This would facilitate communication with the government, he had pointed out. Somehow, the advice was not taken seriously. Did intolerance of the bureaucracy work against Rajan? Or was it the industry and the politicians? Did his being young and being an international figure come in the way? Did we, in the RBI, deserve him? Did we, as a country, deserve him? Many questions, but alas, no answer.

'My name is Raghuram Rajan and I do what I do', was not a mere accidental statement he made at a policy press conference. It was his real self. He did things because he believed in doing them, even at a cost to himself. It is quite sad that he remains misunderstood even today.

7

Does the Institution Need to Change?

There are some policies of the banking industry which the RBI traditionally follows. Earlier it did so for socialistic reasons but now it does it as those policies are too entrenched within the RBI system. It could perhaps be a legacy issue, that somewhere the RBI has been treated at par with commercial banks. The transfer of employees and emoluments for its employees are two such significant areas in which the RBI follows the banking sector.

Every five years, the employees' unions in banks negotiate a revision in their wages with their employers and manage to get a 12–15 per cent hike. This has been happening for more than 25 years now. Once the banking industry wage negotiations conclude, the RBI simply adds a 'central bank premium' to it and settles the wages for its own employees. As the regulator and supervisor of banks, it naturally considers its employees a notch above the other banks' employees in status and, therefore, fixes a tad higher remuneration. That the premium that the government allowed the RBI was negligible and that large banks would quickly add some perks for their employees and make their emoluments better than the RBI's is a different story.

RBI's Transfer Policy

Even transfers came as regularly to the RBI officers as to the bank employees—in three to five years. Albeit, unlike banks, the RBI does not have rural/semi-urban branches; it has regional offices located only in state capitals. Yet, transfer away from Mumbai, the centre for policymaking, was not received enthusiastically by the RBI employees, and they tried to stay put in Mumbai for as long as they could. By changing the nomenclature from chief manager to regional director and calling them the governor's eyes and ears, Jalan did improve their stature and self-esteem, but that was only for the top officers. People at the lower level still felt unhappy.

The unhappiness was because they felt that being away from the top management in Mumbai turned them into strangers for the top management there, and that they would lag behind their Mumbai colleagues in receiving promotions and other benefits, such as scholarships for studying abroad. Jalan did introduce the concept of the regional director briefing the governor on local issues through a monthly one-page letter to the governor. Soon, those letters became longer and lost their 'briefing' character. Even if the governor read them carefully, they did not reach others. I thought these letters had great potential through which the regional offices could share their experiences and experiments among peer groups. I tried to make use of these letters in the fortnightly *RBI Newsletter* whenever I got access to some of them. Though I had requested all regional offices to send a copy of this letter to the communication department and also explained the purpose behind it, initially almost no one shared it as they were meant 'only for the governor's eyes'. But seeing was believing. Those who did share it got coverage in the newsletter, and that encouraged many others to send them to my department too.

Anyway, the reason behind the transfer of bank employees is that they deal in money, and sitting at the same desk for many years brings familiarity, which increases the scope for corruption and frauds. Transfers every three to five years doesn't allow the breeding of familiarity either with clients or with accounts. Unfortunately, this has also become a tool in the hands of seniors to harass juniors or to settle scores. It is not unheard of to see an employee transferred from abroad not to an urban centre, such as a metro city or a tier 1 or 2 city, but straight to a rural area. Is this one of the ways in which the management tries to 'detox' an employee?

There are two points here that I have felt strongly about. First, since, the RBI does not directly deal in money, there is no need for it to blindly follow the transfer policy of banks. Even if the RBI were to implement a transfer policy, its objective should be that of developing a well-rounded officer who can master one or two functions of the central bank—be it supervision, regulation, currency management or even administration. Each function offered wide opportunities for transfers within itself. The regulation and supervision function, for instance, extended across banking, non-banking finance companies and co-operative banks and further to regional offices. The function could also be extended to the foreign exchange department. All these departments are regulatory and offer ample opportunity to the employee to learn the various dimensions of regulation and supervision. Thus, by the time one would have spent 25–30 years in the RBI and come to occupy the decision-making chair as an executive director or a deputy governor, one would have experienced and learnt the entire range of regulatory and supervisory functions to be able to contribute to sensible policymaking. But this was never attempted. Rajan tried to do it but did not succeed much because of internal resistance.

I had another observation regarding transfer. The moment someone got close to being an expert, a transfer order would be on its way. I remember one instance in which I felt really bad about the officer. He was a good officer—knowledgeable and humble. He was developing expertise in anti-money laundering laws and was sought after internationally too. Suddenly, he got transferred to a regional office and was kind of lost there. One day, I saw his photograph in which he was handing out prizes to the employees' children at a regional office function and felt sad.

The approach to transfers could also have put some kind of fear in the RBI officer's mind. No one showed his or her real expertise, always adopting a demeanour of being humble about their achievements. This humility was false. However, there could also be another reason for this sense of humility. Any piece of work was done in hierarchical layers, and so no 'one person' could take credit for any achievement. It was always teamwork, never an individual's work. The fallout of this was that it never allowed the RBI officer to become confident.

The RBI even highlighted transferability in its presentation when it had undertaken campus recruitment. 'Many jobs in one job', the communication said, glorifying transfers among as many as 26 departments and among as many regional offices—as they were called in the 1990s and 2000s. The more transfers the employees faced, the more well-rounded they would be on record. Somehow, there is a belief in the RBI that anyone can do any job.

Developing Expertise

Just by being in the communication department for my entire tenure in the RBI, I was synonymous with communication there. If the external world knew the RBI, it would first be through the governor, and then through me. The media would often say this to make fun of me. I called it an occupational hazard. However, by being in the same function for over 26 years, I was also a kind of memory bank on the communication function. Just as someone else would be in some other department. I see nothing wrong in it. Either you are an expert by education or you learn the job through experience.

Unfortunately, the moment one achieved expertise through experience, one would get transferred to a different department or a regional office. While transfer was an accepted principle, it was often executed with vengeance even at the RBI. There were many cases in which the RBI executed transfers only so that the incumbent did not develop expertise and did not enjoy the benefits deriving out of that, like connections with other central bankers or getting called for giving talks on the subject.

This became even more pronounced when RBI officers started getting opportunities to go abroad for learning or sharing their knowledge in the central banking community. A typical RBI officer would thus be a jack of all trades but master of none. I once called ourselves 'mediocre' in a top-management meeting and there was pin-drop silence for a moment. And then business moved ahead as if nothing had happened.

I remember a time when I had gone to meet a senior RBI official as a journalist. This officer was an expert in his area of work, which was credit. At that time, banks had to refer loan applications beyond a certain amount to the RBI for approval—Credit Authorization Scheme or CAS, as it was known. The officer oversaw that desk. He was simply brilliant and explained the concept of CAS in all its nitty-gritty to me. I was impressed and remember asking him what he was doing in the RBI. His reply to me was that the RBI officers were 'unemployable' elsewhere. I told him that he was grossly mistaken. He only had to step out of his comfort zone to see his market value. The officer later became an executive director in the RBI. Once liberalization set in, many mid-career officers quit the RBI to join the private sector and drew fat salaries. Those who retired also got lucrative offers. I remember a senior officer of the RBI who was also an engineer, who I met after his retirement. He told me that he was making much more money than he did when he was employed with the RBI.

I was recruited to the RBI as a specialist in communication. In fact, I was told when I had joined that the unions had allowed my entry into the RBI only on the condition that I would not be allowed to grow beyond Grade F—the grade of the head of the department. This was because I had joined young—well, young only by the RBI's standard of those times. I was just 32 and had joined as a deputy general manager—the start of the senior management cadre; whereas career RBIites would reach that position only in their 50s. With age on my side, theoretically, I could later claim my stake even for the deputy governorship.

But age is not the only quality required to occupy senior positions in the RBI. The organization is pyramidical. The top is narrow over a large base. Traditionally, in my time, two out of four deputy governors were chosen from within the RBI—one deputy governor from the research cadre and one from the general side. There were seven executive directors at that time. So, that was the highest post an RBI employee could aspire to be at, since the deputy governor and the governor were government employees. Note that, when an RBI employee is selected as the deputy governor, they resign from the RBI and accept government employment.

As executive director and deputy governor, one handles more than one function. The unions reportedly feared that if I was allowed to compete with the regular RBI employee, I might just get the deputy governorship, age being on my side, thus taking away one post from them. Perhaps, they did not realize that handling communication all throughout my career would not qualify me to be even the executive director, let alone deputy governor. It was their perceived fear that got added to my service condition. And I was not promoted beyond Grade F. My personal loss apart, the RBI should analyse the advantages and disadvantages of its transfer policy and reframe it with a view to developing expertise.

Generalist vs Specialist

Another dimension of the averseness towards developing expertise is having two streams of employees—economists and generalists. From their expertise to their designations and their career paths—everything is separate for these two streams in the RBI. Like I have elaborated in Chapter 6, cross-breeding would only bring enrichment to both sides. Worse, the executives encourage such dichotomy and the employees view this as punishment. So, economists posted in general departments would be sidelined and generalists posted in economics department would handle administration. Neither HR nor the top management seriously attempted a reform in this area. Forget merging the two streams, even bringing them together could not be thought of. Simply because so entrenched is this separation in the RBI ethos, that an amalgamation of any kind is extremely complex and, therefore, very difficult. In my opinion, collaboration between the two streams will enrich the work of both.

The Employee Unions

For long, administration and human resources had been under the shadow of unions. There were four unions—one for peons or Class IV, one for clerical staff or Class III, one for Grade A officers who were largely promoted from the clerical cadre and were obliged to be part of their union, and one more for officers in the cadres from B to F, or Class I. Interestingly there is no Class II in the RBI, even for reference.

The story goes that the unions became too powerful when Manmohan Singh was the governor, as he was too gentle a person—more importantly, because he reinstated with back wages a strong union leader who had been suspended earlier by Dr I.G. Patel during his tenure as the governor.

The functions among these classes of employees were clearly defined, and one class could not do the work of another. Unions would ensure that this was strictly followed. The functional delineation was reiterated during strikes. Every morning, Class IV was supposed to come, open the cupboards of the officers, take the files out and keep them on the tables of the officers. Only then could the officers start working.

The dominance of unions was the most visible in the currency department. And if someone tried to act smart, such as trying to do the work that was assigned to another class of employees, the surrounding employees, with the backing of the unions, would teach them a lesson. At times, the 'lesson' resulted in the employee paying up a huge fine or even ending up with a blemish on the career, like currency bundles going missing from their lot, which was a very serious matter.

Jalan demolished the unions' dominance, although I am sure he would feign complete ignorance if asked about it. He, along with Vepa Kamesam, who was brought in as deputy governor from the SBI, quietly introduced mechanization in the currency area and reduced the dependence on Class IV. It was not that they had any animosity towards the workmen staff, but the volume of work was growing phenomenally and deploying machines to do mechanical jobs was the only way to cope with that volume. Computerization also helped demolish the barriers between classes of employees. Since the end of Jalan's tenure, the RBI has not seen a major strike. The salary and perks of the RBI's staff, too, were revised significantly and made respectable in his time. But even he did not try to bring any reforms to the other parts of the administration.

Bridging the Chasm

It was during Reddy's tenure that one economist was posted in each of the regulatory departments. This was not received positively by the staff. To begin with, the research departments posted only those officers who were rejected during the promotion exercise or were not found too amenable—in other words, the ones who were 'dispensable'. So, the research officers posted elsewhere were low on morale, felt dejected, and considered themselves to be outcasts. Naturally, they considered such a posting to be a punishment and lacked any enthusiasm to do something new or different. In the same vein, other departments treated research officers as aliens and not part of the department. Consequently, they were not given their due, or much work. Later, the research department saw this only as an opportunity to create more vacancies for themselves, making it possible for them to get quicker promotions.

Promotion was the other issue over which both cadres remained sore with each other. Generalists felt that researchers got quicker promotions just because they were smaller in numbers, and researchers felt generalists got quicker promotions because they had more opportunities. When I left the RBI in 2019, there were seven executive directors, of which two were selected from the research cadre and five from the general cadre. That meant that only two from research cadre and five from general cadre could aspire to be in the top management. Now there are 11. Still a minuscule number compared to the total number of employees. The pyramid would get narrowed further, as an officer from the research cadre rarely got selected as a deputy governor, on the grounds that they had never been exposed to the real operations area of central banking. Rajan attempted merging the two cadres, and met with very strong resistance. The two cadres continue to remain separate even today.

While the attempt to merge the two cadres did not succeed, the attempt made by governors to develop expertise among the RBI staff met with great success. This included scholarships for research, including doctoral research; doing short-term courses; buying books, computers, laptops; and other such support and facilities. There were schemes for mid-career employees, some of which were brought in to encourage higher studies, and some other schemes to motivate the frustrated staff, as promotion from one grade to another sometimes took as many as 10 years. These included sabbatical and deputation—self-acquired or backed by the RBI. In fact, there were so many schemes and facilities that if one took advantage of all these schemes, one could stay away from the institution for almost their entire career. And there was such a case while I was in the RBI. This officer took advantage of all the possible schemes offered by the RBI. Finally, he even managed to get leave of absence to work at a multilateral institution. It required the late K.C. Chakrabarty, who was the deputy governor in charge of human resources, to take a tough stand by asking all the officers who were in some manner or the other stretching their stay out to either get back or quit the RBI, causing an end to their period of 'enjoying the best of the work opportunities' while enjoying the job security of the RBI. The officer who had stayed virtually all his tenure away, was also given an ultimatum. He resigned but, alas, came back to serve on an RBI research chair in one of the management schools. How he managed so much is anyone's guess; and how the RBI approved so many benefits going to one officer is also strange. Thankfully, this was an aberration. Mostly, the RBI staff benefitted from these schemes and gained knowledge as well as confidence. This reflected in the regulations and research they published.

Moving the Files

Reddy was Jalan's trusted lieutenant in the initial phase of reforms. Together, they brought about not only economic and trade reforms but also significant changes in the way the RBI functioned. Earlier, notes or files moved up and down, sometimes within the entire hierarchy, which was not small—from grades A to F in the officers' cadre, the clerical cadre below and the executive director and deputy governor above. In other words, if the file originated from a clerk, it would move at least eight cadres up and down—from clerk to executive director and back. Naturally, it would take a lot of time before it reached the deputy governor and finally the governor. And most of the time, the hierarchy had nothing much to contribute except for initialling the file and pushing it forward. The person who initiated the note contributed the most, while being the most unsung of the lot.

Much was lost at times because of this. If the bosses did not appreciate what the colleague below had suggested or written, they could just sit over the note and let it die a natural death. There are real examples of such attitude where some bosses returned the notes with some inconsequential remark or a flimsy question. There have been such cases galore. When I joined the RBI, my idea of hierarchy was: when the boss asks a question on file, it should be given utmost importance and immediately responded to. And I did this religiously. I soon learnt, and much to my chagrin, that when the bosses returned the file with a question, it could also mean that they did not want to consider the matter just then or not at all. But rather than saying it on the file, they would play this table tennis match with their juniors.

Jalan was an impatient man and did not appreciate this hierarchical approach, basically because it delayed matters unnecessarily. So the concept of level-jumping was introduced. There were no clear rules for this but it meant that young officers did not have to be at the mercy of their seniors and they could straightaway put up a note to the executive director or even the deputy governor. Reddy himself started meeting the heads of the departments without their executive directors. This was basically to tap untapped minds for creative ideas. Such meetings also served as a means for communicating the rationale of reforms to senior officers. Thankfully, I was invited to such meetings and learnt a great deal.

Being Hierarchical

There are many instances where the RBI showed its typical conservatism and, when nudged, slowly came out of it. In the RBI—as must be clear by now—hierarchy rules. So everyone is a sir or a madam. The first press conference to be called after the credit policy was announced was when Rangarajan was the governor. So, when a youngish journalist asked a question by calling out to the governor as 'Dr Rangarajan', the entire RBI side was shocked. Of course, no one reacted at the conference and it went smoothly, but later, one senior officer asked me, 'Are journalists always so insolent?' I was surprised at the question. In journalism, we called even the editors by their first names. 'Dr Rangarajan' as an address was in no way insolent! But well, here everyone was sir or madam—from peons to senior executives.

It took as long as two decades to get the officials to call each other by their first names. But that, too, happened only among peers. Even now, people of the same age group would call each other sir/madam if they were hierarchically so positioned. It may be that until yesterday, they happened to be colleagues and called each other by name, but today, if one of them got promoted, they would suddenly become either sir or madam. This was unbelievable! What was more shocking was, if not given the due 'respect', the senior would take offence!

It was also a time when the RBI looked like a government office. Old, solid teak-wood furniture in bosses' rooms but for the *aam janta*, the commoners, there were Godrej steel tables, chairs and cupboards. Most women wore saris; very few wore salwar kameez. There was a story about Janakiraman, who later became a deputy governor. He appeared for the interview for the post of a clerk dressed in the traditional South Indian veshti and shirt. He was told by the interview panel that, if appointed, he would have to change his attire. To see someone in any other attire would make heads turn.

The change in the looks—of the RBI as well as of its people—started coming in Jalan's time. He himself came in a bush-shirt and sandals. During his tenure, foreign exchange reserves started building up, and the department that managed the reserves, called Department of External Investments and Operations (DEIO), started getting visitors from abroad. Located on the twenty-first floor, it became the first department to get a facelift. Once that succeeded, the departments queued up for renovation, and today, all the RBI offices and departments have a modern look.

Plain English

There was a time in central banking when 'plain English' was the buzzword. Central bank speak was summarized by Alan Greenspan, ex-chairman of the US Federal Reserve and one of the most revered central bankers. He had famously said in a 1988 speech, 'If I turn out to be particularly clear, you've probably misunderstood what I said.'[7] Central banks were supposed to speak in riddles. Then, along with liberalization, came a phase of transparency which brought about a wave of clear communication. Central banks slowly started moving away from speaking in riddles to communicating in 'plain English'. The RBI also started looking at its communication. Simplification of the language of the monetary policy, and the documents and publications related to it, came first and easily because the governor and deputy governor in charge

[7]Norris, Floyd, 'What If the Fed Chief Speaks Plainly?', *The New York Times*, 28 October 2005, https://tinyurl.com/mr2ub6ea. Accessed on 5 February 2024.

of research and monetary policy were directly involved with these documents. Unfortunately, what we ended up with was reduction in the size and number of these publications rather than making the language more comprehensible.

Admittedly, 'plain English' didn't seem to work for regulatory documents. The Harshad Mehta scam had highlighted, among other things, the lack of clarity in the RBI's circulars. Perhaps influenced by the British, the RBI circulars always used polite language. If it wanted to say 'banks should do…', it would word it as 'banks may do…' Banks generally understood the RBI language, but some would conveniently interpret this as 'not compulsory' to do it. As a result, there was uneven implementation of regulations. There was a sharp comment from the court about this, and the RBI took it seriously for some time and began to consider changing it.

One of the tasks of the Regulations Review Authority (RRA) was to look at simplifying the language of the RBI's circulars, the documents that communicated the regulations to banks. To ensure that they were comprehensible, the circulars, once drafted, were supposed to be read by an officer or a committee of a few officers unrelated to the function. It was also suggested that an outsider—say, an ex-banker—should read the circular to ensure that it was clear in its intent. An ex-banker offered to do this too. But this was not accepted by the regulatory department in the name of secrecy. To begin with, they did not see anything wrong in the circulars, having written those circulars for years together.

This reminds me of two episodes. I had been pitching my services for editing the RBI documents—from its circulars to the annual report—for many years. Deputy governors after deputy governors heard my plea but left the decision to the departments concerned. Nevertheless, they did accept the need to get them edited. The research department, therefore, started getting the publications edited by professional editors as job work. But they did not trust an insider like me to edit them; I had even cleared the test!

Another episode involving the regulatory department was funnier. Jokingly, bankers would say that a typical RBI circular always started with a reference to a circular issued in 1945. It then quoted the subsequent amendments and would, in the last paragraph, say what the change was. So, to know the change one had to dig out all the circulars referred to in the fresh circular and go on putting the pieces together till one came to the latest change. I once suggested conducting a workshop on how to write circulars. To my utter surprise, the suggestion got accepted. I was asked to conduct the workshop for officers as part of RRA's exercise of improving the RBI's communication. I insisted that officers who actually drafted the circulars should participate in the workshop irrespective of their grade. So about 20–25 officers gathered—some of them quite curious, some disinterested, and some even cynical. I began by giving an existing circular to all and asked them to rewrite it in a more user-friendly manner. I did not get much response. When I asked them the reason for their lack of enthusiasm, one senior officer answered, 'Why should I change it? There is nothing wrong in it.' True, there was nothing wrong with the circulars. The RBI could not go wrong in such matters. And bankers had got used to the RBI language. But it could definitely be written in a more user-friendly manner.

That was the whole point. Editing did not mean correction. It meant improvement. Someone could just help communicate in a better way. Why would one not take such help? Was it simply an ego issue? That someone would 'correct' your English was just not acceptable. Here, again, most of the time what was needed to be done to improve the communication was to change the speech from indirect to direct and the voice from passive to active. A typical example was this sentence:

'In this connection, it may please be noted that your suggestion was considered carefully and it is regretted that the suggestion was found to be unacceptable.' I would simply change this sentence to: 'We carefully considered your suggestion and found it unacceptable.' For me, this was a better way to express—not being correct or incorrect.

One good thing that came handy in referencing old circulars was the Internet. The RBI opted to have its own website early on. And that it was placed under the charge of the Department of Communication—at that time the Press Relations Division—worked like a boon for me. I had an absolutely free hand in setting up the website as no one else knew about this technology. Nor did I. I had no choice but to learn about it to be able to make it functional. Fortunately, we appointed a bright young web manager for our website. So, along with the web manager—a very young, bright gentleman, who later became famous for making millions by selling off his Internet portal—I started building up the website. No one was bothered about communication and, therefore, about the website. This gave me the liberty to work with officers who drafted the circulars, access earlier circulars, get them typed and put them on the website with hyperlinks. Slowly, the RBI website grew, becoming a portal and the first reference point for information on banking. In doing so, I was just making the existing information easily accessible. We had still not succeeded in changing the language much.

Only much later did the RBI decisively accept the need to make the circulars user-friendly, and the deputy governor in charge of banking regulation finally took some action. The report, of course, was penned by the officers in the banking regulation department. And I merely shared the mechanics of keeping circulars up-to-date on the RBI website using Internet technology. It was simple. Amend the circulars on a real-time basis on the website using HTML, track change and hyperlinks. How was this achieved? Let us say, a fresh circular is issued today on a subject. Two months later, it gets amended. So another circular is issued amending the original one. On the website, the fresh circular, which is the amendment of the original, will be uploaded as it is, but the original will also show the amendment made in 'track-change' mode. All amendments issued during the year will thus be available on the RBI's website in track-change mode along with the original circular. Those who want to know what the current instructions on that subject are, will just need to download the circular with the amendments in place on their systems, accept all changes, and they will have the current instructions on that subject on their systems. At the end of the year, the department will do the same thing—accept all the changes made during the year and upload the circular on the website afresh—and the cycle will start again.

The idea of simplifying the language, in fact, kept coming up from time to time, but between being technically correct and tenable in the eyes of the law and clarity, clarity always took a back seat. And so, the suggestion of writing the circulars in plain English was never accepted in its entirety. The result is that the language of the circulars remains complex even today!

Epilogue

As I have said earlier, each governor got over the so-called weak area of the earlier incumbent. Venkitaramanan started the reforms in the RBI but needed a longer tenure to make a difference in real terms. Unfortunately, media bashing did not allow that to happen. Next came Rangarajan, whose credentials were impeccable on controversial issues. He was an economist and could be sticky on economic issues, but was absolutely non-controversial on other issues. Jalan, who succeeded him, was a practical and flexible person. These qualities took care of the stickiness of the economist, particularly with the bureaucrats. He was particularly lucky as during his time, despite several crises around the world, Indian economy buoyed and its foreign exchange reserves started to swell. He could, while leaving the RBI, confidently say that 'India will never face a foreign exchange crisis again.'

After him came Reddy, who was like Lord Krishna. Unbending on principles but flexible with their implementation—a tenure full of solid work and action. Then came Subbarao who, after Reddy's high-pitched battles with the government, had a rather calming effect, at least during his first term. His tenure was preoccupied with fighting the most severe global financial crisis and celebrating the platinum jubilee of the RBI. Rajan, who followed him, was again unbeatable on subject matter. His tenure also was full of hectic activity, mainly on management of banks' NPAs. He unfortunately got brandished by the media as the governor who 'talked too much'. Urjit Patel, who succeeded him, believed in working quietly. This was initially well appreciated but soon started to be perceived as arrogance. Later, he also got mired in a bitter battle with the bureaucracy and decided to quit, citing personal reasons. Shaktikanta Das, who came after Patel, is an IAS officer, and knows how to balance the walk with the talk. He knows how to keep the government and the media both on his side and, so far, his tenure has been quiet and non-controversial.

The governors who came after the year 2000 were somewhat different from the ones before. Be it Subbarao, Raghuram Rajan or Urjit Patel, they had studied and worked abroad and had imbibed much of the Western culture. Calling each other by first names, using American phrases in everyday parlance, and their somewhat informal and non-hierarchical approach in the office were characteristic of them. They abhorred the security officer who travelled with them every day from home to office and everywhere else. Some showed disdain and others tolerated it with grace as a professional hazard. Jalan managed to do away with the armed security officer and instead got a plain-clothed security officer to accompany him. Subbarao and Rajan accepted the presence of the security officer with some reluctance. At some point, the lal batti on the governor's car was done away with. But all of them refused to let someone else carry their bags, even when they travelled. Patel went one step ahead and stood in the queue for check-in at the airport carrying his backpack. He completely did away with the security personnel accompanying him from home to office and back.

One fallout of the status was their restricted personal freedom. Jalan loved to go for movies, plays and concerts and eat at good restaurants. He would do that quite often. Invariably, someone—not necessarily media—would spot him and take a picture, and we would see it on page 3 of a newspaper the next day. Initially, I felt that for a traditional central bank, the governor appearing on page 3 of *The Times of India* was quite weird and was avoidable. After giving it some thought, however, I realized that the governor was human after all and must have some personal freedom. So I did not get worked up about page 3, except that one time when one socialite called Rajan 'James Bond' in a pink paper.

Adjusting the Timings of Press Conferences

The advent of television channels on the scene required some tweaking in the media policy that I followed after each monetary policy announcement. Earlier, we used to have the policy announcement in the morning and the press conference in the afternoon. Television channels would telecast the press conference live but they had to cut it off at 4 p.m., as that was the time for their news bulletin to give the market round-up.

The press conference, at that time, would go on for more than two hours, as, after Mumbai, we would connect with the other three metros to speak to the media there. That was made possible by Webex technology, which had arrived on the scene sometime during the mid-nineties. Once again, we were among the first ones to adopt this technology for our policy communication—much before Covid-19 happened and popularized this form of virtual meeting. As against gathering in our regional offices, which used to happen earlier, regional media could now connect from their own offices and from their own phones. The use of Webex technology also facilitated transcripts of press conferences. We could upload the audio in a few hours after the press conference and, a few days later, even the transcript of the press conference would go on the website for later reference by markets. Market and media both benefitted from and appreciated this initiative.

However, between the policy announcement and the press conference, there was a long gap of about three to four hours, even if they were happening on the same day. During this gap, the analysts and media would start analysing the policy, which could, at times, lead to miscommunication or a focus on a lesser point of the policy. So, we tried to insert a small session in between in which the governor and a deputy governor would give a sound bite to the television channels. Governors and deputy governors were ever-obliging. The sound bite conference also engaged the non-business channels, which would usually withdraw from the scene after getting the bites, leaving mainly the business channels behind. This also facilitated interaction with the print media; they were otherwise always cribbing about the cameras and crew of television channels obstructing their access. The short session in between took care of all these in one go.

Later, we shifted the press conference to a slot immediately after the announcement of the policy. Thus, we successfully guided the public attention to our communication before they could hear other voices. The top management would speak to the analysts later in the afternoon. This initiative went extremely well among the analyst group, whose market-related technical questions got answered in detail. Some central banks from the Western world also showed interest in doing a similar conference.

From News Summary to Market Intelligence

When I joined the RBI in 1992, we used to get some 20-odd newspapers in our division. Apart from reading them, I do not quite remember what else we did with those newspapers at that time. But reading them took almost half of my day. Venkitaramanan's speed of reading was phenomenal. So, even as I would be barely awake in the morning, he would call me up to tell me about some news item appearing in one of the newspapers and discuss it with me. Most of the time, I would draw a blank, as I read the newspapers after reaching office. Although he never told me so, he would have found me quite useless in this matter. Once, I saw him read an office note, and his eyes moved vertically over the paper and not horizontally. I would be stunned at the speed at which he used to finish reading the note and give his decision.

Since he paid so much attention to newspapers, I made it a point to read them carefully. But that mostly remained wishful thinking because my reading would invariably get overtaken by some urgent work, and the newspaper would lay half-read on my table with some page open through the entire day. The next day, it would have turned to nothing but *raddi* (waste), as they say. I would feel miserable, as all those newspapers stacked up unread outside in the division.

I was once complaining about this to a friend, and he suggested a solution to this problem. He said that, as far as he could guess, no one in the organization would be getting all those newspapers or would have the time to go through them. His idea was that I should make a news summary and circulate it among all the departments. I liked the idea and started doing it.

I added a clippings service for the top management. We clipped important news relating to the RBI and banks and sent the clippings to the top management. One good thing about the RBI was that no one would stop you from doing something new, as long as you did not step on someone else's toes or spend money. I also started building a library of relevant cuttings. I would, at the peak of the Harshad Mehta scam, mark every small detail of the scam in all the newspapers, and someone would cut and stick the lot neatly on plain papers and file them. This was also required to feed the informal committee we had, to prepare the governor on the issues that could be raised by the JPC that was investigating matters relating to the scam. We sent the files later to the RBI archives, and I hoped that someday, someone would access them and do research.

The initiative wasn't appreciated at first. I even saw the news summary we created being used as lunch paper, as it was called. If you ate your lunch at your own desk, normally you laid out some paper on top of the table and then opened your lunch box on it so that the table did not get spoilt. That paper was called lunch paper in the RBI! Anyway, marking the newspapers and writing an intelligible summary of the major news items started taking too much of my time, as I would read the news and then summarize the relevant parts in my own words. We could send out the news summary to executives only by afternoon, which was too late. To be able to send it before lunch, I handed it over to one of my junior colleagues and taught him the job. He was smarter than me. Instead of writing the summary, he started marking the first paragraphs of the selected news. This was mostly fine, but not always. But, for lack of more resources, I had to accept this. At least, we could send the news summary to the top management a bit earlier.

Much later, we thought of outsourcing the service. Not many service providers were available in the market for this kind of service, though. So, initially, I simply taught the job to a vendor, who gave us one original set and four photocopies to be circulated among the governor and four deputy governors.

They all appreciated this initiative. I could see this, as the sets would come back to us after the top brass had seen the clippings. Sometimes, some copies would have markings made by the governor or deputy governors. At times, there would be some remark or action point for some department on a clipping. And we would send those to the relevant departments for further action.

I never followed up on what action the department took, as I thought it was not my job. But what was gratifying to know was that a service we had started to justify the purchase of so many newspapers was slowly evolving into market intelligence. Yes, the first step towards having a market intelligence unit in the RBI was the newspaper clipping service provided by the Press Relations Division. The RBI would often get news or unknown information related to individual banks through newspapers, which was useful for the Bank in its supervisory role. Tarapore would often ask me how, as journalists, we gathered news. Meeting relevant people was crucial for news gathering, as people who you know well would often share information with you. Taking a cue from this, a unit of three young officers was set up. Their role was to meet relevant people and gather news that would be useful in the RBI's supervisory role. This was called the market intelligence unit.

Seeing the success of this service, I wanted to make it more efficient and effective. The first thing was to computerize it. Sending the news summary with hyperlinks, by clicking which one could see the newspaper clippings, would have made the service easier and quicker. But to my utter shock and surprise, the executives refused to let me go electronic, with hyperlinks to the actual news clippings. They did not want the service on email. They only wanted hard copies so that they could mark them and send them to the departments for further action.

Those were also the early days of computers and not many knew how to efficiently use the machines. Nevertheless, we kept looking for a professional service.

Many years later, we found two such international-level service providers who were being used by other central banks too. After much struggle, we succeeded in onboarding one of them. We worked with the agency to bring the service as close to what we used to provide to the management and finally started emailing the news summary. Once we had the service in electronic format, the next step was to send the news summary to all the RBI employees. Why not? After all, everyone has a right to information!

Foreign Wire Agencies

The media's affection and trust in me was sometimes overwhelming. Their goodwill for the RBI as an institution was telling. We learnt from one another and did many things together. The operationalizing of the embargo was entirely done in consultation with the wire agencies. Foreign wire services played a crucial role in telling me how things worked in central banks around the world and how we could modulate that to suit India and the RBI.

Together, we also tweaked the rules for releasing market-moving press releases and publications with an embargo. This enabled the media to read the release carefully, understand the communication, rewrite it if necessary in their own way and release it at a pre-notified time. This made the RBI communication simpler for their readers to understand.

Foreign wire agencies' work ethics are worth emulating too. They make sure to talk to all the parties involved in a story. If any party does not speak to them or speaks anonymously, they make sure to mention that. Basically, they make sure they do not do a one-source story. They make their editors and reporters accountable. They also give the utmost respect to the central bank of the country and try not to invite the central bank's wrath onto them.

Despite that, such a thing did happen a few times in my career in the RBI. Once, a foreign wire agency did a story which quoted a deputy governor. This caused a little flutter in the market. The deputy governor, however, denied he said any of what he was quoted for. The wire agency insisted the deputy governor was quoted verbatim. But the deputy governor completely denied saying anything of the sort. So, we issued a denial.

Going by the rules, the wire agency ought to have published the denial just as they had published what he reportedly said. But they did not—even after my telling them that it was our prerogative to issue a denial and they ought to publish it. I also told them that if they so believed in their version, they could publish their denial to our denial. But the agency just refused to oblige. With the managment's approval, we had to ban them for a week from getting any news from the RBI and did not send them any press releases during that time. Of course, they still took it from our website. Since we were updating the website in real time, the agency could file the news a few seconds later than the others. I am sure the editor was called to explain this internally, as he kept pleading with me to restore their privilege. I was able to do it only when the stipulated week of punishment was over.

Next time around, the same agency was not so lucky. For something that displeased the top management of the RBI, a ban was imposed on it. Two of their reporters were banned from entering the RBI for filing a story that we thought was not based on facts but on gossip. The ban on the agency was lifted after some months, but it continued on the two reporters. One reporter was later transferred to Delhi and the other was taken off from the central bank beat. I am not sure if this was the repercussion of the ban but for the reporters concerned, the charm of reporting was gone. That is what they told me later.

Another wire agency was banned for reporting something that was shared with them on the understanding that it was not for reporting. This time the ban was against the reporters and not against the agency. They remained under ban for quite a few months.

Cut-Throat Competition

Seniority and promotion in the RBI were two hot subjects of discussion among officers. We also used to publish, for internal use, a seniority-wise list of officers. So cut-throat was the competition that they would always keep looking at this publication to see how far they were from the next promotion. This would sometimes take a sad turn. Once, it so happened that a senior officer who was in charge of a regional office of the RBI had come to Mumbai for some work. He was on his way back to the airport when he suddenly suffered a heart attack. Before the cabbie could do anything, he passed away. The news spread like wildfire. Among the chatter that went around was also the question of the seniority list—who moved how many places up in the seniority list? It was quite common to see one-time colleagues becoming seniors and juniors to each other.

This was a regular phenomenon in the RBI and, I am sure, is also the case in the government; or, in fact, in every large organization. It happened because there was a time when the government looked upon every public sector undertaking, including banks and the RBI, as employment-creating units. Like banks, the RBI also had to recruit people on a mass scale—in batches of 500–700. Like in the government, in the RBI, too, people belong to batches. These lots belonged more or less to the same age group and got their promotions more or less at the same time. But as one went higher, the opportunities became fewer and competition among the same batchmates became tougher. Once an officer entered the senior management cadre, that is, the post of deputy general manager, his one eye remained on the seniority list to know when his turn for the next promotion would come. The promotions, largely, were seniority-based. If for any reason the officer who was above someone moved out from the list, it would be a matter of great joy for the next person, expecting that their number would come earlier than listed.

Wishes Unfulfilled

Even though I was very happy with the way my career shaped up in the RBI, and I was instrumental in changing the way the RBI communicated, I had my own hits and misses. In my entire career in the RBI, I worked closely with the governors and dealt with many a crisis. With each new governor and deputy governor, I would make a case to let me edit the RBI publications or get involved with writing the history of the RBI. But I did not succeed in either. However, subsequently, we did employ historians and a journalist to write the history of the RBI. This meant that the management did realize the need for editing and writing the RBI publications in plain English to make it accessible to the non-technical public.

Very few know that in the very first year of my career, I had put in my papers out of sheer frustration. This was partly my fault, as I had perhaps expected that I would bring about a revolution and change the whole institution. I was obviously wrong. Institutions are built over years and decades and have their own history and behavioural pattern. No one, not even the governors, could change it overnight. I was far too junior and small to do it. Naturally, I got frustrated. Thankfully for me, the governor at that time, Rangarajan, and Deputy Governor Tarapore understood my frustration. Tarapore counselled me about how a large institution like the RBI worked and asked me to rethink my decision. Rangarajan told me that if I decided to stay back, he would involve me in writing the live history of the RBI. Both, however, left the decision to me. Of course, I did not get into the history project, as Rangarajan was too preoccupied with the reforms that were being undertaken at the national level, with the RBI doing its bit at every stage. But I did change my decision and withdrew the resignation, only to leave the organization after some 26 years with my retirement!

Hierarchy and Its Ways

I believe that in a hierarchical organization like the RBI, every dog has his day. Only, one has to wait for one's time. Today, your boss could suppress your voice; but tomorrow, you might be the boss, and be able to voice your view freely. It is noteworthy that in an institution made of technocrats, like the RBI, one could also voice one's views fearlessly. The policy notes invariably travelled both ways—upwards and downwards. One could always add one's view on that note and it would become and remain a part of the official record. Whoever wished to counter that view also had to do it in writing on that note; that, too, would become part of the official record.

The discipline of such a hierarchy was that while one had the freedom to freely convey one's views internally, once the final view was taken on the issue, everyone was required to carry that view through to the outside world. The institution could punish you if you didn't. Many such cases have occurred in the past; it's just that they were not very high-profile and therefore did not get publicized.

Interests of Specialists

Over the years, the promotion scheme was changed many times, but none could satisfy the majority. And so, disgruntled elements always existed in the RBI. The voice of specialists was feeble. I was not the only specialist in the RBI! There was a whole Legal Department, along with engineers in the Premises Department, which even had a qualified architect. Later, there were librarians, archivists and curators for the RBI museums. These specialists needed to be nurtured with reasonable promotion policies and incentives, such as the scholarships and trainings abroad that were available to the regular RBI fraternity. But it was already difficult to manage the two branches of employees—economists and generalists. Adding the specialist category to these would have only complicated the promotions and functioning. But yes, there ought to be HR policies clearly laid out even for specialists.

Being a specialist had caused me a couple of more losses. There was a scheme in the RBI under which a few bright chief general manager- (CGM)-level officers were rewarded with a one-month incentive to study in any university in the world. This was a fully paid learning opportunity. I never received this incentive. When I once asked my senior why I was never considered for a nomination, I was told that it was because I was a specialist, and specialists did not qualify for the incentive. When I pointed out that in the same year one engineer CGM, who was also a specialist, was given the incentive, I got no response. When I asked HR, the response was, 'your senior needs to nominate you!' Was it a case of the crying baby getting the milk every time and that I never cried?

At a much younger age, and a few years into the RBI, I had applied for a study abroad under the RBI's Golden Jubilee Scholarship Scheme. Studying abroad was my lifelong dream. The RBI had introduced the scholarship scheme in its fiftieth year to encourage its employees to pursue research. One had to apply for the scholarship, but there was tough competition, as only five people were given the scholarship. Research in central bank communication, which was my subject, would stand low in the list of priorities. Yet, apply I did. At the interview, the executive director in charge of the research department asked me questions related to my work, insinuating that I did not bring any change in the way the RBI communicated. At a formal panel, I could not openly say that my vision for the function was gathering dust on one of the deputy governors' desks. The external panelist tried to save the situation by telling the executive director that he should ask me questions on my statement of purpose for the research. But the executive director was hostile. It was clear to me in the interview itself that I would not be selected for the scholarship. I never applied for it again. Sometimes, I do think that I should have applied again after that executive director had retired. My taking the episode negatively cost me a big opportunity that could have helped me enhance my skills.

Demonetization

With Rajan's exit, I was entering the last phase of my career. My last two years in the RBI stand apart from the rest of my career. With each governor, I had to shift gears and adapt to different communication strategies and practices. With Urjit Patel, however, I had to completely change the direction of my journey.

But not before I took care of another once-in-a-lifetime event. Shortly after Patel took over as the governor, the government announced the demonetization of ₹500 and ₹1,000 notes. This was demonetization, or de-mon, as it was nicknamed by the media.

We were working on the new designs of currency notes quite some time before Patel took over. This was quite a normal activity as central banks the world over keep changing the designs of their currency notes almost every ten years. This is to keep ahead of the forgers or the copycats. The central banks keep researching on security features that are difficult to copy. With technology, such features keep evolving and get added to the existing currency notes. They get a complete overhaul every 10–12 years. Normally, the notes with old designs also remain in circulation when the new designs get introduced. So, the general public does not have to worry about the new and the old. But demonetization is a different game altogether. When a certain denomination or denominations of notes get demonetized, the government orders these to be withdrawn from circulation from a particular date. This affects the general public directly, as they have to exchange the demonetized notes with current notes within a stipulated but short time.

Currency notes are demonetized basically for two purposes. Either the notes are rampantly counterfeited or people hoard their black money (unaccounted income on which tax has not been paid) in these denominations. Both forgers and hoarders generally focus on high denominations. Economists normally do not support demonetization, as the loss to the general public and the economic activity is far more in this case than its gains. The decision to demonetize, therefore, is taken in most cases by the governments, and its gains are almost invariably political.

When we started working on the new designs of the notes, there was also a thought of introducing a new denomination. We did not have enough denominations in the series of two. We just had currency in the denomination of ₹2 and ₹20—even if ₹2 was no longer available as a note, it was still available in coin form. Research showed that denomination in the series of two facilitates public transactions. Let us say you have to make a payment of ₹500 to someone; you can either give five ₹100 notes or one ₹500 note. But if there was a denomination of ₹200 in between, one could pay with two ₹200 notes and one ₹100 note. The discussions with the government about the denomination and design were ongoing. We were looking at a denomination of ₹2,000 to begin with and then ₹200. We were working on the designs of ₹2,000 with utmost secrecy. There were infrequent rumours in the market about demonetization and the introduction of new denomination in currency notes, but there was no confirmation to the rumours—neither from our side nor by the government. These rumours became stronger in 2016—still no confirmation from authorities. I would generally brush the topic aside when the media turned to me to fact-check the rumour.

One evening, at around 8 p.m., as the office was closing and I was preparing to leave, a journalist friend called. He told me that the government had announced demonetization of ₹500 and ₹1,000 notes. I told him that such rumours had been circulating in the market for some time now, but there was no solid base to these assumptions. He told me to look at the television, on which the prime minister was making a statement. The television set in my office room was always on but on silent. As I turned towards the television, I could read the scrolling headline. The news was correct! I could barely absorb the news before my telephone started ringing. From that moment, until the next day and beyond, my phones never stopped ringing. Journalists would call to find out and understand the implications of the new notification that had been issued. In fact, notifications were being issued almost every day, and I had to run faster and faster just to keep up with new information coming out of our currency department. There was no briefing. I was assimilating all information alongside the public through the notifications. The only advantage I had was I could understand the meaning of the RBI circulars faster and better because of the years I had spent in the institution.

The RBI drew a lot of flak during this time, but we had decided not to talk on the subject. And rightly so. To demonetize was the government's decision. Now, it is in the public domain that no central bank can be in favour of demonetization. In fact, most economists would not support it. The government was well within its power to overrule the RBI and go ahead with demonetization, which it did. Since it was the government's decision, it was up to the government to explain its decision to the public, and the role of the RBI was merely that of a good soldier and to carry out the commander's orders in the best way possible.

This needs to be understood well. The RBI is a technocracy. The governors and the deputy governors of the RBI are appointed by the government. The government is elected by the people of India. Naturally, the RBI will be subservient to the government, as the top management of the RBI is 'appointed' and not 'elected'. In any case, as a sovereign, the government is above all authorities. Further, the Reserve Bank of India Act, under which the RBI is set up and draws all its powers, provides for the government to 'overrule' the RBI's decisions by issuing 'directions' to it. So it was indeed the government's prerogative to announce demonetization, even if it meant overruling the RBI.

On 8 November 2016, when the decisions to demonetize ₹500 and ₹1,000 notes and introduce a new denomination of ₹2,000 notes in a new design were announced, we had to release two advertisements—one related to the new design, and the other one a press release announcing the decision of demonetization and what the public needed to do. This was a couple of hours' work, as we already had the advertisement related to the new designs ready. But I could leave office only on the morning of 9 November, having spent all my time answering the questions of the anxious public. There were incessant telephone calls from the media and even the general public, seeking clarifications on the action required of them. People had doubts. My phone number was somehow available online and people used it unhesitatingly at that time to call me directly.

There was one chartered accountant who asked a lot of questions that were tax-related. I answered them all. I do think my answers were convincing, as after the 40–45 minutes of conversation he sounded satisfied. Of course, I had to clarify to him that the RBI had no jurisdiction over tax matters and that I had answered these questions based on my general knowledge and common sense and that he should rightfully check with his tax consultant for advice. He then told me that he himself was a chartered accountant and that I had answered all his queries correctly!

I had received no briefing on the subject before the decision was announced. Naturally, such a big decision had to be kept a secret; otherwise, the purpose of demonetization would simply get defeated. So I had to carefully read the notifications that were being issued. Once in a while, the department which was spearheading this huge drill would help out. And, in a rare moment, the deputy governor in charge of this task would brief me. Everyone was busy and always in a rush against a deadline. The media was hungry for news, and, if no news was available, they busied themselves creating controversies. Since we had decided not to speak on the matter, the media kept asking me to give them information informally or off the record. But without any brief or briefing, I could barely do this.

There were many queries and many stories till about February–March of 2017. Most of them were related to the suffering of poor people. Some stories were of intrigue and others of pure anger.

This one was from Kolkata. It was narrated to us by a colleague who was posted to oversee exchange of currency notes. The last date for exchanging the notes for Indian residents was over. But a visibly poor, young man—maybe in his early twenties—would come and quietly stand in front of the RBI's Kolkata office every day. Others in the crowd would shout, try to throw their weight around, just so that the RBI would relent and accept their currency notes. There was no way the RBI could do this as that would mean breaching the law. One day, out of sheer curiosity, one officer went to the young man and asked him why he came every day and stood in front of the RBI. Apparently, the young man and his poor mother had been hiding money in the bamboos which made the roof of their hut in their village. They were saving to make a new house. By the time they got to know about demonetization, the date for exchange was gone. Their savings, which were somewhere around one lakh rupees, had turned into junk paper. Our heart bled at such stories, but we could do nothing. People would curse us, and all we could do was hear them out. Some of our young officers would tell me, 'Madam, we must have sinned in our last birth; that's why we have to go through such misery.'

Next came the NRIs. Many Indians had flown down from overseas just to exchange their currency notes. But there were rules put in place by the government and the customs authority that needed to be followed. Not many NRIs were fully aware of all these rules. The RBI rules were clear and available on the RBI's website. However, few understood them correctly. For instance, there were separate rules and deadlines for exchange of demonetized currency for NRIs and for people with overseas citizenship of India (OCI) status. What was not clear to the public was who was an NRI and who an OCI. People of Indian origin but who had surrendered their Indian citizenship to embrace another country's citizenship were not entitled to exchange the notes under this clause. The deadline for their exchange had passed along with that for resident Indians. They could have had all the papers required for the exchange, but they were still not eligible.

Since our task was to collect the notes that were deposited with us, we would collect them alright, but we could not replace them with new notes after the deadline had passed. Further, the value of the exchange was supposed to be deposited in the bank accounts of the depositor. Unfortunately, a large section of people who deposited their cash were ineligible for exchange because they were neither NRIs nor OCIs as per the law. Some did not have a bank account in India. Some came without collecting the custom department's certificate from the airport which would prove that the currency notes were indeed brought by the NRIs from abroad and not collected from an Indian resident after coming to India.

There was no one place where the NRIs could get full information on exchanging the notes. They felt cheated. They thought the RBI was not helping them and that there was something fishy in the way it was handling the whole matter. They felt the RBI was collecting their hard-earned money and not returning it, only to put it into its own kitty or the government's. Miscommunication was rampant. This could have been avoided by coordinating clear communication to begin with. We could have included the definition of NRIs and OCIs in the press release itself. All information related to the requirements for exchange of notes could have been put together as an information kit, and made available at all the branches of Indian banks abroad, at the airports, and other places of significance, so that the NRIs knew exactly what was to be done.

There were many stories in the media about how people tried to get around the law. Some of them were not even written due to lack of proof, but journalists would tell me about these. For instance, there were these agents who helped with the exchange of notes at a price. They would tie up with groups of people who moved from one bank branch to another exchanging currency notes for agents. The agents would give them food, water and some cash to do this. Since there was no system-wide check or restriction, much cash got exchanged like this. Then there were small shops which, among other things, recharged phones. Since they could deposit ₹2 lakh a day in demonetized currency, they became a medium for exchanging demonetized currency notes. There were stories galore of housewives and old folk losing their hidden cash.

With an almost everyday change in instruction, we were seen in a very poor light. Some even called us the 'Reverse Bank of India' as we were issuing a certain instruction one day and reversing it the next. This was a strategy, I was told. We had to deliberately first tighten and then relax the rules, just so that genuine people got the benefits and the rogues would be fearful. How could such a strategy be explained to the public? So, we took all the criticism in our stride. We had perhaps foreseen every move that happened on ground. Reportedly, this was also explained to the government in as much detail before the decision was taken. And yet, the government decided to demonetize.

Creativity...Finally

The opportunity to do some creative work suddenly landed in my lap after Raghuram Rajan left. A senior and bright officer was posted in the communication department. The officer was action-oriented. He relieved me of all day-to-day work. Administration and media relations usually took almost 80 per cent of my work hours, leaving me hardly any time for any creative work. We had, on our hands, two huge projects—one, to create a museum for the RBI, and the other, a public awareness campaign on RBI regulations on the customer service of banks. These had not progressed much because of my preoccupation with day-to-day work.

Both administration and daily media calls, which occupied most of my time as the head of the department, were now out of my hands. I could finally focus on both these projects. I also had the support of a young and energetic team to help me in these. Both projects finally took off. By the time I hung my boots, we had fully rolled out the public awareness campaign 'RBI *Kehta Hai*' (RBI Says), and the RBI Museum in Kolkata was ready for inauguration. Both the projects were challenging and highly creative. Once again, except for the required approvals, I had absolute freedom in carrying out their execution. Both the projects were very satisfying and were my swan songs—literally. I feel happy to have left a legacy behind for generations to come.

As I stepped out of the RBI, an economist of repute commented, 'End of an era.' Indeed! An entire generation changes every 26 years. But I firmly believe in *mujhse behtar kehne wale*. There will be better storytellers than me. I do hope that the RBI takes the function forward from where I left it.

Good luck, RBI!

Acknowledgements

Who all should I thank? Should I thank them only for this book or for all that went behind this book? Or should I go even further and include those because of whom I have received all that I have in my life? The list will be long. But let me try. I extend my gratitude to:

Ex-Governor Venkitaramanan, for extending me an opportunity and the push to start the RBI journey, and to Dr S.L. Shetty, the then economist at the RBI, for making me think about joining the Bank.

Ashok Advani, the publisher of *Business India* magazine, who encouraged me to join an institution like the RBI to learn about banking and finance, even if he had to let go of a good employee.

All the governors, deputy governors and my other senior colleagues and peers from whom I absorbed knowledge like a sponge.

My girl gang in the department who so keenly heard all my stories while at work and kept telling me to write them down (lest I forgot them!) in the form of a book, which I always laughed off but ultimately got down to doing. And here is the result.

T.C.A. Srinivasa Raghavan, whose rap on my knuckles finally got me down to writing. He even suggested the title for the book!

But then started the difficult part of the journey—writing—for which I must thank my family. My gratitude to Varsha, my sister, who has always nudged me to maintain balance between my capable self and my frivolous self. My nephew Vimarsh and his wife Ami prodded me, most of the times silently but sometimes even aggressively, to complete the first draft. Once I finished writing the first draft, reviewing and finalizing it was much easier. Not to forget my younger nephew Tanay and his wife Ashleigh—my gratitude to them for their affection.

How can I not thank Dr Reddy, who so readily and unassumingly wrote the foreword? And Dr Rangarajan and Dr Subbarao, for so willingly agreeing to write an endorsement for the book?

In Rohan Datta and Aditi Mehrotra of Rupa Publications, I found more than just editors. They taught me editing all over again! Their alert minds and extra careful eyes have made me improve my expressions at many a place, making the book near error-free.

And ultimately, my father and mother, who always felt very proud of the smallest of my achievements. I am sure, today, they would feel the greatest joy to see this book come alive.

My gratitude to all of them.

Index